The Wisdom *of*
His Compassion

*Meditations on the
Words and Actions of
Jesus*

Joseph F. Girzone

ORBIS BOOKS
Maryknoll, New York 10545

Founded in 1970, Orbis Books endeavors to publish works that enlighten the mind, nourish the spirit, and challenge the conscience. The publishing arm of the Maryknoll Fathers and Brothers, Orbis seeks to explore the global dimensions of the Christian faith and mission, to invite dialogue with diverse cultures and religious traditions, and to serve the cause of reconciliation and peace. The books published reflect the views of their authors and do not represent the official position of the Maryknoll Society. To learn more about Maryknoll and Orbis Books, please visit our website at www.maryknollsociety.org.

Copyright © 2009, 2012 by Joseph F. Girzone

Published by Orbis Books, Maryknoll, New York 10545-0302.

All rights reserved.

No part of this publication may be reproduced or transmitted in any form or by any means, electronic or mechanical, including photocopying, recording or any information storage or retrieval system, without prior permission in writing from the publisher.

Queries regarding rights and permissions should be addressed to:
Orbis Books, P.O. Box 302, Maryknoll, New York 10545-0302.

Manufactured in the United States of America.

Library of Congress Cataloging-in-Publication Data
Girzone, Joseph F.
  The wisdom of His compassion : meditations on the words and actions
  of Jesus / by Joseph F. Girzone
     p. cm.
ISBN 978-1-57075-971-0 (pbk.); e-ISBN 978-1-60833-140-6
   1. Jesus Christ—Person and offices—Meditations. I. Title.
BT203.G57 2009
232.9'03—dc22
                                    2008019766

Also by Joseph F. Girzone

THE HOMELESS BISHOP

JOSHUA

JOSHUA AND THE CHILDREN

JOSHUA IN THE HOLY LAND

KARA, THE LONELY FALCON

THE SHEPHERD

NEVER ALONE

JOSHUA AND THE CITY

WHAT IS GOD?

JOEY

A PORTRAIT OF JESUS

JOSHUA: THE HOMECOMING

JESUS, HIS LIFE AND TEACHINGS

THE PARABLES OF JOSHUA

THE MESSENGER

TRINITY

JOSHUA IN A TROUBLED WORLD

MY STRUGGLE WITH FAITH

JOSHUA'S FAMILY

Contents

ACKNOWLEDGMENTS

xiii

FOREWORD

xv

THE ANNUNCIATION: A VISITOR FROM HEAVEN

1

SORRY, NO ROOM

6

ANGELS APPEAR TO SOCIAL OUTCASTS

10

Contents

A Visit by Very Important People

14

The Refugees

17

A Young Jesus Comes of Age

21

He Takes upon Himself Our Burdens

26

Forty Days Harassed by Satan

31

No Prophet Is Honored by His Own People

36

It Is Not the Time My Father Had Planned

43

Want to Please God? Be a Child

49

Don't Embarrass God When You Pray

53

Contents

Why Did You Have to Wake Me?
58

The Publican with a Clean Heart
61

Would You Hug a Leper?
64

The Law Was Made for Man, Not Man for the Law
67

The Pagan Soldier with a Humble Heart
71

When We Condemn, We Are Condemned
75

We Judge by What We See on the Outside; He Judges
by What He Sees in Our Hearts
80

When You Pray, Pray to Your Father in Secret
87

It Is Our Sins That Entitle Us to His Mercy
91

Contents

The Excommunicated Holy Man

95

Who Will Be Invited to Live in God's Home?

99

Moses and Elijah Surprise the Apostles

104

If You Want to Lead, Learn to Serve

108

What a Strange Choice as Messenger of the Good News

112

Don't Be Discouraged If Success Comes Slowly

118

The Prodigal Father

122

I Need to Be Alone

127

Violence Does Not Resolve Issues; It Breeds Nightmares

133

DO WHAT THE SCRIBES AND PHARISEES TELL YOU,
BUT DO NOT IMITATE THEM!

136

HIS WAYS ARE NOT OUR WAYS

139

NO REST FOR THE WEARY

144

STORM CLOUDS OVER THE LAST SUPPER

149

KEEP FORGIVING IN SPITE OF YOURSELF

153

IT IS NOT HOW MUCH YOU MAKE THAT COUNTS,
BUT HOW MUCH YOU GIVE AWAY

157

"WHY WAS THIS NOT SOLD TO HELP THE POOR
RATHER THAN WASTE IT ON HIM?"

161

ONE MOMENT OF GLORY

165

Contents

THEIR LAST SUPPER TOGETHER

170

———

THE SAD LAST NIGHT

175

———

SUNRISE ON A DARK NIGHT

181

———

SURPRISE!

187

———

SEEING IS NOT BELIEVING

191

———

GOOD-BYE, BUT I AM NOT REALLY LEAVING

195

Acknowledgments

For the Scripture passages quoted throughout this book I used as a basis translations in the New Jerusalem Bible and the New International Version, though the quotes are not exact but my paraphrasing of them.

I would like to express my gratitude to Maggie Carr and Sean Mills, who did such a marvelous rendition of the original manuscript by polishing so many of the rough edges of my very earthy writing style.

I am also deeply grateful to my dear friend Trace Murphy, my editor for so many years, and for his encouragement and expertise in producing excellent finished products of all my books, especially this present one. I am also greatly indebted to Darya Porat, who is always there when I call and has been such a help in difficult times.

Foreword

I have studied and meditated on Jesus' life during most of my life, and after all these years I am beginning to realize how little I know about Him. I wish I had a thousand years more with the hope of learning more about Him, but even then I would be not much further along in understanding the impenetrable depths of His inner life and the feelings of His heart. His mind is like a vast mine filled with precious gems of every possible color and shade and brilliance that can never be fully explored, much less penetrated. His mind is as wide as the universe, His love as deep as the heavens and just as incomprehensible. Human love has needs that demand fulfillment. Jesus' love needs nothing but knows only how to give. To the human way of thinking that kind of love is not only incomprehensible, but unreasonable. People imprisoned in rigid concepts of

God learned from childhood, or people who are afraid to go beyond literal meanings, will never be able to understand that kind of love. A good example is Jesus' vivid story of the prodigal father, a story that we have always called the parable of the prodigal son. In this parable Jesus tries to reveal to us the vast difference between His Father's love and human love. For the father in this story, the thought of retribution or punishment does not even cross his mind. His longing for his son's return is all that concerns him. It seems almost an obsession, as the father looks out across the horizon all day long hoping to spot his returning son in the distance. And when his son does return the father runs out with his servants to welcome him; the father does not even ask if his son has learned his lesson. Indeed, not just this story but the whole Gospel story seems one unrelenting attempt by Jesus to help us understand the unfathomable love of His Father.

In this little volume I am painting word pictures of Jesus, to show in each snapshot a different insight into the wide-ranging facets of Jesus' personality. I hope it helps us all to understand a little better the way He looks upon us weak, frail human creatures, and to see that in our God to whom we have looked with awe and wonder and so often with fear, there is also a remarkably warm and compassionate personal divinity. But that compassion should not be mistaken for maudlin sentimentality. It needs to be understood as an expression of God's wisdom and understanding of our frailty as humans. People are sometimes too prone to see in God a God of punishment and retribution, failing to realize God's chief desire, which is always to heal, thereby viewing punishment and retribution as more reasonable. If people don't believe in a loving, merciful God, they are more likely to be judgmental, brutal, and unmerciful to others. I hope this study of Jesus will help us to see the wisdom of His compassion.

Fr. Joseph F. Girzone

THE WISDOM OF HIS COMPASSION

The Annunciation:
A Visitor from Heaven

[The angel Gabriel] said to Mary, "Hail, full of grace. The Lord is with you." But she was greatly troubled and was trying to understand the meaning of such a greeting. And the angel said to her, "Do not be afraid, Mary, for you have found favor with God. And I tell you, you are to conceive in your womb and bear a son, and you are to name him Jesus. He will be great and will be called Son of the Most High. The Lord God will give him the throne of David his ancestor. He will rule over the House of Jacob forever and his kingdom will have no end." Mary said to the angel, "How can this be since I have no knowledge of a man?" The angel answered, "The Holy Spirit will come upon you, and the

> *power of the Most High will cast his shadow around*
> *you. And the child will be holy and will be called*
> *Son of God. And I tell you further, your cousin*
> *Elizabeth, now in her old age, has conceived a son,*
> *and she who was considered barren is now in her*
> *sixth month, for nothing is impossible to God."*
> *Mary said, "Behold, I am the handmaid of the Lord.*
> *Let it be done to me according to your word."*
> LK 1:28–38

CYNICAL PEOPLE WILL READ THIS PASSAGE AND EIther laugh at it or shrug it off as a mere mimicry of Greek or Roman mythology. If a person with faith who believes the story tells it to a person without faith, it is not hard to imagine the response. I wonder if Saint Luke, who was an educated Greek doctor, had any difficulty with the story when Jesus' mother first related it to him—and she is the only one who could have told him. It seems he accepted it and believed it sufficiently to make it part of his Gospel. The simplicity of Mary, as well as her humility, is impressive. The angel's prophecy about Mary's cousin Elizabeth is a stunning revelation. Elizabeth and her husband, Zachariah, lived over ninety miles away, and it seems there is no way Mary could have had any knowledge of Elizabeth's condition without the angel telling her the secret.

Mary's concern for her elderly cousin shows her humility. Her remarkable eagerness to go and offer help to someone in need demonstrates her willingness to serve others. A less humble person would have expected others to wait on her. But there is none of that in Mary. She is surprisingly self-effacing, and seemingly unaware of the honor that has been bestowed on her. Indeed, it was her humility that gave her the strength to live with the cruel cynicism of neighbors and even relatives who could in no way look upon Mary's predicament as an extraordinary blessing from God.

If cynics still think that the story is fabricated, they need only look at the later life of Mary's Child, and if they have an open mind Jesus' public life should dispel any doubt that God was mysteriously and powerfully involved from the very beginning in His life on this earth. No other being in the history of the human race could work the miracles and raise the dead, or equal in any way the sublimity of Jesus' whole existence here on earth, including His ideas, which far transcended anything ever taught in all of recorded history. Why should the beginning of His life here on earth be any less sublime, and how could it not be touched in an extraordinary way by God?

Saint Augustine, as did many of the Fathers of the Church, referred to Mary as the second Eve. God offered some very special gifts to our first parents, gifts that they were to have passed on to us. But Eve and Adam rejected

God's offer and lost all the treasures we should have inherited. Because God has such respect for the free will He gave us, He does not demand things of us; He *asks* us. Love cannot be demanded. It must always be a free choice. So God sent a messenger to ask Mary if she would consent to become the mother of His divine Son. Saint Augustine, in commenting on this scene, said that at that moment the destiny of the human race hung in the balance. If Mary had said no, we might not have had a savior and might not have been saved.

There is a mystery here. God asks something special of each of us. He has special things planned for us if we are willing to cooperate with His love. We can say yes or no. He wants us to touch the lives of others, many others. If we respond to God's call the lives of many others will be deeply touched and changed in ways we could never imagine. If we say no, I would rather not think of what might follow. Adam and Eve said no and lost for their descendants the precious heritage God had planned. As for Mary, we all owe a great debt to her for having consented to bring to us our Savior. It is a shame that so many Christians choose to shun her. I wonder what her Son thinks of that. If my friends were to treat my mother that way, I would find it hard to consider them my friends.

The meeting between Mary and Elizabeth is fascinating to contemplate. Their relationship seemed most cordial. How closely related they were is not mentioned in the Gospels. The angel was aware that Mary knew Elizabeth and Zachariah, and that she would be impressed to find out that her cousin was pregnant—an interesting piece of gossip coming from an angel! Forgetting all about herself, Mary made preparations to go and spend time with her elderly cousin, knowing she would be needing help. From the joy and thrill of their seeing each other it is clear they were already very dear friends. When they hugged and their bodies touched, Elizabeth felt a powerful sensation in her womb. The baby did not just move. He "leapt," as if touched by God's Spirit, as the Scripture says, to recognize the presence of his Savior. And Elizabeth herself said under the inspiration of God, "Who am I that the mother of my Lord should come to visit me?" How profoundly moving to see the intimacy of God so powerfully present at that moment as these two saintly women embraced! Perhaps the angel also told Elizabeth about Mary or perhaps God revealed it at that moment. Whatever, under the inspiration of God, Elizabeth recognized that Mary's little embryo, only weeks old, was already the living Son of God.

Sorry, No Room

And Joseph also went up from Galilee, from the city of Nazareth, to Judea, to Bethlehem the city of David, because he was of the house and lineage of David to be enrolled with Mary, his wife, who was with child. And while they were there, she gave birth to her firstborn son and wrapped him in swaddling clothes and laid him in a manger, because there was no room for them in the inn. LK 2:4–7

THIS IS THE FAMOUS CENSUS WHOSE EXISTENCE historians used to question until over fifty years ago a tablet was excavated that stated that a census was to be taken up all throughout the Roman province of Syria.

Joseph and Mary traveled by caravan the ninety miles to their ancestral home. It can be presumed that there were still some relatives of Joseph's living in Bethlehem. There surely were relatives who had returned there to register for the census. Whatever the situation, Mary and Joseph were unfamiliar to any of them. One would expect that somebody with an ounce of human kindness would pity the poor young mother about to give birth. No one seemed to care. The manager of the caravansary, a stranger, was decent enough to realize that this open-air motel filled with animals and rough travelers was no place for a young mother to have her baby. He kindly suggested that there would be more privacy in a cave down on the hillside. There the couple could at least be alone and safe from the prying eyes of crude strangers.

And that was where the child was born, in a damp, chilly, and smelly cave. His crib was a feeding trough from which animals ate their grain and hay. The warm breath of the donkey may have provided a few degrees of warmth. His mother's embrace gave Him His real warmth and security. I got a brief hint of an infant's insecurity recently when I had hurt my back and the pain left me totally helpless. Being alone that one night I could feel how insecure and helpless a baby feels when separated from his mother, whose body provides warmth and food and security for nine months. Being away from his mother's womb and on his own is a terrible experience; he craves his mother's warmth and embrace yet can do nothing to obtain it. The feeling of being alone and disconnected can be terrifying. Childhood fears begin at that early age and have to be soothed away to help the infant to know security.

Fortunately, one of my sisters and her husband stayed with me the next night and for a number of nights until I could fend for myself. Just knowing that there was someone nearby was such a comforting feeling.

Even as an infant Jesus had His first experiences of the insecurity and helplessness we experience, the anxiety that goes along with being separated from one's mother's body, and for the first time being alone. It was His first experience of being human, His first experience of the fear humans sometimes feel. Some may doubt this, but when one of my brothers was being born he fought so hard not to be born that even the doctor was shocked that a baby could be so frightened at the prospect of leaving the security of his mother's womb.

Lying in the manger was the first time Jesus felt what it is like to be cold. What a shock, to learn what life is like for us. He would have many more shocking experiences so He could learn what it is that drives us to do the things we do, including the often strange and evil behavior we engage in. It was His own experiences that made it possible for Him to have compassion for us.

How long did the holy family stay in Bethlehem? It is not certain, but in the story of the Magi the Gospel mentions that when they came to pay respects to the newborn King, they found the family in a house, and not in a cave. Based on the information the Magi gave Herod, he ordered his soldiers to kill all the baby boys under two years old. The holy family could have been living there for a year or more. The trip back to Nazareth would have been a long way for a newly born child to travel, so an extended stay in Bethlehem makes sense.

Angels Appear to Social Outcasts

And in that region there were shepherds keeping watch over their flocks at night out in the field. An angel of the Lord appeared to them, and the glory of the Lord shone around them, and they were struck with fear. The angel said to them, "Do not be afraid. I bring you tidings of great joy for all the people, for to you is born this day in the city of David a Savior who is Christ the Lord. And this will be a sign for you: You will find a baby wrapped in swaddling clothes and lying in a manger." And suddenly there was with the angel a multitude of the heavenly host praising God and saying, "Glory to God in the highest and on earth peace to men of good will."

When the angels left, the shepherds said to one another, "Let us go over to Bethlehem and see this thing that has happened, which the Lord has made known to us." And they found Mary and Joseph and the baby lying in the manger. When they saw this they told everyone what had been told them concerning this child, and all who heard it wondered at what the shepherds told them.

But Mary kept all these things in her heart. The shepherds in the meantime returned, glorifying and praising God for all that they had heard and seen, just as it had been told them. Lᴋ 2:8–19

AGAIN THERE IS NO OUTSIDE EVIDENCE OF THIS OC-currence other than the story as related by Mary to Luke when he was writing his Gospel. We believe it based on our acceptance of the honesty and integrity of Jesus' mother. If we cannot believe her, then no historian could ever be accepted as credible. Some Scripture commentators may debunk this story as concocted by the evangelists, but these commentators promote their theories without ever offering solid evidence that a particular Gospel story is not historically true. In time many of their theories are proven wrong. So, until someone comes up with evidence that a particular Gospel event did not occur, the Gospel story still stands.

Jesus' whole life was so intimately tied up with God in

such extraordinary ways, and the power of God was so clearly evident throughout His life, why should anybody, much less a scholar of Scripture, be bothered by a simple story about His heavenly Father's announcing to simple shepherds the good news of His Son's birth?

Jesus would later thank His Father for having revealed to the simplest children what He had kept hidden from the proud and the clever. The story of angels announcing Christ's birth to simple shepherds—people who were outcasts from their religion because they lived lives among the animals, and thus were prevented from observing all the rules of their religion—is so much in keeping with the attitude Jesus was to manifest so often later in life. The story fits so perfectly into the spirit that Jesus was to portray during His later life as He cared for the sinners whom the scribes and Pharisees excommunicated from the temple.

The simple shepherds could not contain their joy but had to tell the whole neighborhood what they had just experienced. Their simplicity itself lends to the story's credibility. The story also shows the Father's preference for the poor, simple people whom Jesus also favored. It might seem more logical for God to announce the Messiah's coming to the religious leaders, since they had been prepared to recognize and accept the Son of God when He came. He knew they could not be trusted to believe the revelation, much less handle it as sacred, but these simple, unwashed shepherds He could trust, first of all to believe the message and then to handle the message with reverence and humility as they told the whole world around them.

That simple story of the shepherds coming to visit the Infant Savior is still one of the most moving scenes as we renew the Christmas celebration each year.

A Visit by Very Important People

Now when Jesus was born in Bethlehem of Judea, in the time of Herod the king, wise men came from the East to Jerusalem, asking, "Where is he who has been born king of the Jews, for we have seen his star in the East and have come to worship him?" When Herod the king heard this he was troubled, and all Jerusalem with him. Assembling all the chief priests and scribes of the people, he inquired of them where the Christ was to be born. They told him, "In Bethlehem of Judea, for so it is written by the prophet, 'And you, Bethlehem, in the land of Judah, are by no means the least among the rulers of Judah, for from you shall come a ruler who will govern my people Israel.' "

Then Herod summoned the wise men secretly

*and ascertained from them when the star first ap-
peared, and he sent them to Bethlehem, saying, "Go
and search diligently for the child, and when you
have found him, bring me word so I too may go and
worship him."*

*When they had heard the king they went their
way, and to their surprise, the star which they had
seen in the East went before them, till it came to
rest over the place where the child was. When they
saw the star they were filled with joy, and going into
the house they saw the child with Mary his mother,
and they fell down and worshipped him. Then
opening their treasures they offered him gifts of
gold, frankincense, and myrrh. And being warned
in a dream not to go back to Herod, they departed to
their own country by another route.* MT 2:1–12

SOME SCRIPTURE SCHOLARS DOUBT THE EXISTENCE
of the Magi, theorizing that the Gospel writers made
up that story too. However, coins recently discovered in a
remote section of Iran, formerly Persia, had engraved on
their faces the head of a king named Caspar, which was
the traditional name of one of the Magi. The other kings
were Melchior and Balthasar. The archeologists also found

the remains of the building where Caspar lived. Later, when Saint Helena, the mother of the Roman emperor Constantine, was on an extended pilgrimage in the Holy Land, her excavators found the cross on which Jesus was supposedly crucified. When news of this find spread to Persia, the king sent a precious gift to Helena: the remains of King Caspar's body, which Helena brought back to the church in Milan where she had been baptized. The story about the Magi may not be as far-fetched as it might appear. In the writings of the Zoroastrian religion, there is a remarkable prophecy that when the Jewish Savior comes His star will appear in the east, and people should go with gifts to honor the newborn Savior of the Jews. My attitude toward the Gospels has always been to accept what is written in them until scholars give solid evidence that something is not historically accurate. Theories calling into question events recorded in the Gospels are no substitute for cold, hard facts.

The Refugees

When the Magi departed, an angel of the Lord appeared to Joseph in a dream and said to him, "Rise, take the child and his mother and flee to Egypt, and remain there until I tell you, for Herod is about to search for the child, to destroy him." And he rose and took the child and his mother by night and departed for Egypt, and remained there until the death of Herod. This was to fulfill what the Lord had spoken through the prophet: "Out of Egypt I have called my son." MT 2:13–15

SKEPTICS HAVE A FIELD DAY WITH THIS STORY, AS there has been no way to verify that this event ever occurred. There were no witnesses that the Holy Family left Bethlehem to escape from the mad king's jealousy. Critics even deny that there was anything like Herod's slaughter of the innocent children of Bethlehem since there is no outside source to verify it. Again, these critics hold that the Gospel writers added the story to make it look like another prophecy about the Messiah was being fulfilled which said that "Out of Egypt I have called my son."

The trip from Bethlehem through Gaza and the Sinai desert to Egypt, as told in Matthew's Gospel, raises very colorful images of this long-suffering couple and their child who had, since the very beginning of their life together, undergone so much pain and hardship, now taking a lonely trip into exile as refugees. And this was just the beginning.

While nothing is mentioned in the Gospels about the Holy Family's stay in Egypt, there is an amazing wealth of information about their stay in Egypt, much of it the product of legends and stories passed down among the people, the Muslims as well as the Christians. The Egyptian government today even proudly marks out and updates the route which local traditions hold was the route the Holy Family traveled while moving from place to place in Egypt. The government is quite proud to point out, not just the highway, but the places associated with the Holy Family's stay in this present day mostly Muslim country. They themselves embrace these shrines and make pilgrimages to them. The shrines belong to the Coptic Christians, who long ago built them and through some nineteen centuries restored them after they had been damaged or vandalized. Descendants of Coptic Christians, whose ancient families were converted by Saint Mark the Apostle in the latter part of the first century, still pass on the stories and legends of what happened in each of these places where Mary and Joseph and the Child spent part of their time while in Egypt. These Coptic Christians, groups of whom recently reunited with the Catholic Church, still offer the sacred liturgy with the same rituals taught to them by the Evangelist Saint Mark and his associates almost two thousand years ago.

One might ask, what is the value of dwelling on the journey to Egypt and the time spent there? Its value is again in the experience of Jesus, taking His lessons on our own experiences, our own pilgrimage through life. Refugeees have always been a very big part of the human experience through the centuries, and for the most part not always welcome by their new hosts, as we are just learning in our own country being inundated by refugees from hunger and starvation in their own countries south of us. In Egypt at the time of the flight of the Holy Family, there were almost a million Jews, mostly around Alexandria. It seems they were well treated, but many of them were well educated and as professionals were rather well-to-do. A simple couple like Mary and Joseph were unknown and alone, and it does seem that making a living may have been difficult, and explains why tradition has them traveling from one place to another to eke out a simple livelihood.

Jesus had many memories from His earliest childhood to carry with Him, and become a part of His understanding of what people undergo in their lives here on earth.

A Young Jesus Comes of Age

When he was twelve years old they went up to the Passover festival as usual. When the festival was over and they were returning home, the young Jesus stayed behind in Jerusalem without his parents knowing it. Assuming that he was somewhere in their caravan, they went a day's journey and then began looking for him among their relatives and acquaintances. Not finding him, they returned to Jerusalem in search of him.

After three days they found him in the Temple area, sitting among the teachers, listening to them and asking them questions. Everyone who was listening to him was astonished at his understanding and his responses.

When his parents saw him, they were overcome

> with emotion, and his mother said to him, "My
> child, why have you done this to us? Don't you
> know that your father and I have been worried sick
> looking for you?"
>
> "Why were you looking for me? Didn't you
> know that I must be busy about my Father's work?"
> But they did not understand what he meant. He
> then went back with them to Nazareth, and was
> obedient to them. His mother stored all these things
> in her heart. And Jesus grew in wisdom and in
> stature in the eyes of God and his townfolk.
> Lk 2:42–52

A T TWELVE YEARS OLD JEWISH BOYS WERE CONSID-
ered adults, and this particular Passover festival may
have been the occasion of Jesus' bar mitzvah, when He
became a "son of the Law." Conscious of His new status as
a legal adult, He knew He now had responsibilities. He
obviously was somewhat if not totally aware of His identity
with His Father in heaven and felt it His duty as an adult
to become involved in His Father's interests. Precocious
Child that He was, and an independent adolescent, He
decided on a course of action without even considering
His parents' wishes or plans. He could not wait to test His

knowledge of the Scripture, which He had learned at home and from wandering scribes who regularly visited rural synagogues, against the teachings of the Scripture scholars and legal experts associated with the Temple. They were the real professionals, the aristocratic and scholarly priests with high standing. This bright young man was thrilled to be allowed to ask questions and even respond to the questions of these teachers. As learned as they were they must have been stunned at this mere boy's extraordinary grasp of Scripture and the Law, and more so at His ability to cut through nonsense and aim right at the heart of the law and the meaning of the prophecies.

After hearing their son's voice somewhere in the vicinity and following it till they found Him, His mother and Joseph, I am sure, did not barge into the area where the scholars were holding their session. Out of sheer curiosity they would have stood off to the side and listened to what their son was saying to these scholars. They were, like all the others listening, stunned at the wisdom that poured forth from this child's lips. His mother never forgot it, and kept it in her heart, wondering what it all meant.

One's heart cannot help but go out to this mother who could never totally understand the mystery of the child she was raising. It is difficult enough raising an ordinary child, but the mystery of raising God's son, whatever that meant to her, would have been unfathomable. How would you handle such a child, especially as He began to show awareness that He was in some special way related to God in heaven? How does a mother cope with such an awesome responsibility along with the panic at the thought of having lost Him in the big city?

Did the parents just sit in as the session continued or did they immediately excuse themselves and take the young boy with them? The scholars probably asked them to stay and hear what their brilliant son was saying, assuring them that they would be proud. Whatever happened, eventually they did leave and Jesus humbly and obediently went back with them, as Mary obviously told Luke later on when she was relating these events to him. From then on Jesus was a respectful and caring son, growing daily in wisdom and in the admiration of their small circle of friends and neighbors. His experiences conditioned Him to understand the joy and sorrow in the lives of the people He loved. His later sensitivity to people's pain of loss was probably awakened in Him during those tender years as He saw His stepfather, whom he dearly loved, becoming sick and showing signs that he would not be with them much longer. The pain He must have felt in losing someone so close to Him had to awaken in Him compassion for the pain we all feel when we lose loved ones. He always showed sympathy for a family losing a loved one, particularly a child, as He did for the widowed woman at Naim, who was burying her only son. As He grew He was constantly learning what it was like to be human and feel the pain of human suffering, and our feelings of anxiety and helplessness.

As He got older He became more and more aware of what we all go through and how we feel when we have high ideals and yet fail to attain them. Even though He could not sin, He could understand our sense of failure in our feeble attempts to live good lives. These experiences built up the extraordinary understanding of human frailty He was to show later on.

He Takes upon Himself Our Burdens

Jesus came from Galilee to John at the Jordan, to be baptized by him. John, trying to stop him, said, "It is I who should be baptized by you, yet you come to me to be baptized." "Let it be for now, for all justice must be fulfilled," Jesus responded. MT 3:13–15

THIS SHORT PASSAGE REVEALS SO MUCH. JESUS' baptism is an official public act. For ordinary people, being baptized by John was an occasion for them to confess their sinfulness and be baptized as a sign of repentance. For Jesus to undergo the same ritual would have been looked upon by bystanders as a confession of sin. His baptism may have entailed a confession, but the sins He was admitting to were not His own. He had come, as Isaiah prophesied, to take upon Himself the sins of us all. He came to represent all of us and to take upon Himself the burden of us all.

One of the most difficult parts of my life as a priest has entailed asking myself daily how Jesus would treat this person's or that person's problems or serious sins. In developing the habit of thinking like this, one becomes more and more identified with Jesus as the Good Shepherd who carries the burden of people's pain and sins. So many times people advise priests, "Don't get emotionally involved with people's problems." Easy enough to say, but if you are a priest trying to be like the True Shepherd, your heart begins to beat like the heart of Jesus, who once remarked, "I feel sorry for the people; they are like sheep without a shepherd." Then He walked up on the hillside and talked to them into the early evening about their pain and their fears.

When we read that Jesus took upon Himself the sins and burdens of us all, it is not just a nice saying. Jesus really felt the burden of our sins and our pain. When He healed someone, power went out of Him, as it says in the Gospel when the sick woman touched the hem of His robe and was healed. Healing is stressful for the healer, and Jesus healed all day long. It was not just an occasional gesture; it was his daily work. As soon as He appeared in a village, the crowds brought Him all the sick and lame from the surrounding area to be healed. And He healed them all, not just a few here and there. I began to understand not just the mind, but the heart of Jesus after many years of contemplating Him, living with Him, as I was taught as a young Carmelite friar. He could not come across a person hurting or in pain and just walk away. He felt that person's pain. Having the heart of God and seeing into the heart and soul of each person He met He could immediately feel the burden of their lives, the burden of their sins, and the burden of their pain. As I grew older as a priest I began to understand that about Jesus, and because I was gaining a deepening understanding of the almost universal damage done to people going through life, I was feeling their pain more and more, and I carried it with me when I prayed and when I offered Mass each morning. My Mass became a desperate plea to the Father, an offering through Jesus of the unbearable pain of those committed to my care and of the suffering people throughout the world.

I began to see more clearly the pain Jesus carried with Him all His life, not only His own pain, but the anguish of all those He met along the way. He expressed His understanding of His role among the people one day, when He described Himself in the figure of the shepherd in search of a lost sheep as the "Good Shepherd" in contrast to the mentality of the scribes and Pharisees, which could be paraphrased, "I am the Good Shepherd. I go out in search for the lost, the troubled, the bruised and hurting sheep, and when I find them I pick them up, place them on my shoulders, and carry them back home." He's not talking about only physical pain. He is talking about sinners who are bruised and hurting and troubled, who feel lost in their guilt.

He is concerned for them because He feels their pain. He went out looking for them, searching high and low until He found them, because He knew they were hurting. We are not used to thinking of God as feeling our pain, but Jesus makes this known to us. He worries about us. He does everything He can to comfort us. So many people think that God is the reason that we suffer. God doesn't plan to make us suffer. It is often we who bring suffering upon ourselves. God tries to help us bear the suffering, and if we let Him He tries to bring good out of our pain and our sins.

There is a mentality today among some religious people that the Church would be better off if its membership fell off to just a remnant consisting of those who keep the rules. That is no different than the elitist attitude of the scribes and Pharisees who continually excommunicated those who could not measure up to all that the religion demanded. They felt very comfortable with a more observant remnant. But the Good Shepherd, who describes Himself as the one who loves the sheep, went out to search for all those whom the Pharisees considered rejects, and upon finding them He picked them up, placed them on His shoulders, and lovingly carried them back home. So many good people, including many clergy, miss that whole drama that Jesus describes when He talks about the Good Shepherd, whose attitude toward His flock is the opposite of what He saw in the elitist attitudes of the religious leaders of his day.

One truth is certain. When we suffer we do not suffer alone. Jesus always suffers with us, and He carries in His heart the burden of our pain and our sins.

Forty Days Harassed by Satan

And Jesus was led into the desert by the Spirit to be tempted by the devil. MT 4:1

SAINT PAUL WRITES THAT JESUS WAS LIKE US IN ALL things but sin. In this passage we see Jesus in the desert being tempted by Satan. Were these real temptations that could affect Jesus and present a real problem for Him, or were they just superficial encounters with a creature who could in no way pierce the divine armor of the God-man? There are many good believing people who don't believe that Jesus was really tempted. "How could God be tempted? Especially by Satan, if he is even real?"

Jesus was like us. He had a body and a soul. There was

a human part of Him. He learned the way we learn. He had feelings like we have. He could feel the pangs of hunger. He could suffer pain. We see Him crying on a number of occasions. We see Him tired and depressed. We see Him so scared that He sweat blood. We see Him hurt when after He had cured ten lepers of their hideous disease only one came back to thank Him. We see Him sensing His failure as the Messiah when He wept over Jerusalem. He had wanted so much to bring these people back into His Father's love, but they would have no part of Him. We see Him hurt when the apostles could not stay awake and comfort Him when, broken in spirit, He desperately needed the solace of their love and friendship.

Yes, He could be tempted. There were dreams He wanted to see fulfilled more than anything, but He chose to restrain all His divine power and limit Himself to using only the human resources at His disposal. What a temptation it must have been when things were going wrong to know that He could resort to supernatural powers that could in an instant accomplish what He willed! Was He tempted to destroy those self-righteous scribes and Pharisees, or at least neutralize them and show the people that even those powerful leaders were no obstacle to His sacred mission? To Him they were no more than irritating flies on a muggy summer day. But He reserved His extraordinary powers not for Himself but for those who were sick and crippled and blind and possessed by evil spirits. He did not use them for His personal convenience. He liked the good things we like, He loved parties, and He could desire the things we desire, but He denied Himself these things when He deemed them improper or incompatible with His mission.

When people could not understand His message, how often was He tempted to touch their minds or their wills and make them understand? The apostles themselves were very dense. Even after being with Him for three years they still could not comprehend what He was doing or who He was. How frustrating! It would have been so easy to expand their limited intellectual powers so they could see clearly all He was trying to teach them. And He was oh so patient, trying everything to help them see and understand, for instance, when He tried to teach them humility in exercising authority. After overhearing them arguing among themselves over who was the greatest among them, He told them that whoever wanted to be the greatest must be willing to be the servant of all the rest. Even at the Last Supper, still concerned about how they would treat people after His departure, He got on His knees and washed their feet, hoping to set an example of humility for them since His words had failed to change them.

Jesus knew what it was to be tempted. That is why He can understand our temptations. He has compassion for us when we succumb to temptation because He knew from His own experience how difficult it was to resist and never give in. We are fortunate to have a God who understands us, even when we do give in to temptation.

And those temptations by Satan in the desert were real. Satan knew that the time for the Messiah's coming was imminent but he had no way of knowing who would be the Messiah. He tried desperately and in a most cunning manner to tempt Jesus into revealing His identity. Satan said, "Your fast is ended. You must be hungry. You have no need of starving yourself any longer. Your hike back to the city is long and the day is hot. If you are God's Son, take one of those stones and turn it into a loaf of bread, so you will have the strength for the journey. You don't want to collapse on the way."

"It is not by bread alone that man lives, but by every word that comes from the mouth of God," was Jesus' noncommittal response.

Then taking Jesus up in imagination to the pinnacle of the Temple, where he could fall hundreds of feet below to a valley of rocks, Satan said to Jesus, "If you're the Son of God, throw yourself down. After all, it is written in Scripture, 'He will give his angels to support you, lest you stub your toe against a rock.'"

"It is also written, 'You shall not tempt the Lord your God,'" Jesus said.

Satan was getting nowhere.

Then in a conjured up image he took Jesus up to a high mountain and showed Him all the kingdoms of the earth. "See them all. They're all mine, you know. But I'll make a deal with you. If you are the Son of God, you have come down to win the hearts of all these souls. Not an easy task, well-nigh impossible. But I will relinquish all my control over all these people and allow you to accomplish your mission in one brief moment. Just fall down and worship me, just once, and they will all be yours."

"Begone, Satan. It is also written, 'The Lord your God alone shall you worship and Him alone shall you adore.' "

Satan had more than met his match. He still did not know who Jesus was, nor had he been victorious in his sly confrontation with Him.

Yes, they were real temptations. Jesus could feel the poignancy of the enticements. He was hungry. He knew He could count on the angels to protect Him if He so chose. He knew how impossible it would be for Him to win the hearts of everyone, but He also knew what a liar Satan was. So in disgust He drove Satan away, although Satan would return to tempt Jesus on later occasions.

No Prophet Is Honored by His Own People

And he came to Nazareth where he had been raised, and entering the synagogue as was his custom on the Sabbath, he stood up to read. The attendant handed him the scroll of Isaiah the prophet. Opening the scroll, he found the place where it was written, "The Spirit of the Lord is upon me; he has anointed me to bring good news to the poor, to preach liberty to those in captivity, to give sight to the blind, to release those who are oppressed, and to announce the favorable year of the Lord, and the day of recompense." Then rolling up the scroll, he gave it back to the attendant and sat down. The eyes of all in the synagogue were fixed on him. And he began to say to them, "Today this scripture has been fulfilled in your hearing." LK 4:16–22

And those who heard him were astonished, and said, "Where did he get all this wisdom and these miracles from? Is not this the carpenter's son? Is not his mother named Mary, and are not his brothers James and Joseph and Simon and Jude? And his sisters, are they not all with us? Then where did he get all this from?" And they took offense at him.

Jesus said to them, "A prophet is not without honor except in his own country and in his own house." MT 13:54–57

I HAVE ALWAYS STRUGGLED WITH THIS PASSAGE AND with the event itself. It reveals so much, yet it is so confusing because it raises so many questions about Jesus' place in the minds of the townsfolk with whom He had lived for almost all of thirty years. He has just come back from a journey to Judea, during which He insisted that His cousin John, the baptizing prophet, baptize Him. He apparently spoke on a number of occasions and healed some people while on that journey, because word to that effect reached His neighbors in Nazareth. They were bewildered. They must have thought, We didn't know He could do these kinds of things. At the synagogue that Sabbath He spoke to all his neighbors, and they were impressed by his sudden burst of knowledge. "Where did He get all this from, and His miracles as well?" They apparently had never seen anything like this in Him during all those years they had known Him as He was growing up.

I have tried to analyze what Jesus' image was in the community as a young man. The question "Where did He get all this from, his wisdom and his healing powers?" made me realize that there was something changed in Jesus on His return to His hometown after He had been baptized. We know Him as the Messiah, and as the Son of God. In all the years He lived in Nazareth, the people certainly did not look upon Him as the Messiah. They certainly had not the slightest idea that Yahweh had been living in their midst in a human form for all those years.

One thing that really troubled me was that the people apparently did not look upon the young Jesus as particularly holy, because they were so shocked when they heard He had been speaking about spiritual things and working miracles on His recent trip to Judea. All those years growing up in Nazareth He had not impressed His neighbors as being particularly holy; that's strange because He had to be the holiest person who ever walked this earth. I asked myself why the people did not see this. Then I realized that for a Jewish person, holiness meant keeping the Law, all the Law, the whole 613 commandments of the Law, and the 365 prohibitions, and the 365 lesser prohibitions. If a person received high marks for being super-observant, he would be considered holy. Jesus apparently did not have a reputation for being particularly observant. Why? For good reason. He knew most of those mandates were not from His Father but had been concocted by the scribes and arbitrarily placed on the backs of the people, who in turn found it impossible to observe them. So He just ignored most of the rules as irrelevant to healthy human living.

What then did the people see in Jesus? They saw first of all an attractive young man, active, energetic, hardworking, partnering with His stepfather in earning a living to provide for the family, and perhaps the extended family of aunts and uncles and cousins living with them, and maybe even a couple of grandparents. They would have seen Him as very intelligent, brave, and not afraid to speak His mind whether others agreed with Him or not, basically afraid of nothing. They would have seen that He had a very healthy way of looking at life, a far-reaching vision of things as they might unfold in the future. He was strong, physically, and manly, partially due to the demanding kind of work He and His stepfather did each day. At the same time He was emotionally sensitive and very gentle. He also had to have a remarkable sense of humor because He could easily see the many odd and outrageous antics among people in the neighborhood. In short, the people saw in Him a person deeply in love with life and everything alive from God down to the simplest living creature, a beautifully well-balanced human being Who must have been a lot of fun to be with. It is not hard to imagine that many of the girls in town might have been secretly in love with Him. After all, for all they knew, He was just one of them.

So now to the incident in the synagogue. What happened there on that Sabbath morning? Matthew said that Jesus had been speaking in the synagogues in the area, and the people were astonished. On this particular Sabbath He attended His hometown synagogue. When He got up to speak, the people already had a bad attitude, and even though they were amazed at His newfound wisdom, no matter what He said it would not have softened their bad attitude. Probably it was because He had not preached to His townsfolk first and had not worked miracles among His own people; they had to find out from strangers that He had all these secret powers. He did honor His townsfolk, however, by announcing to them for the very first time that He was the Messiah, that Isaiah's prophecy was being fulfilled right in their very sight. Hearing that should have made them proud, but instead the announcement went right over their heads. Seeing their hostile looks, He brought the issue right to the surface. "No doubt you would like to say to me, 'Physician, heal yourself! Work here the miracles we heard you have been working in other places.' In truth I tell you, no prophet is ever accepted in his own country."

They were infuriated and they dragged Him out of the synagogue and brought Him to the edge of town intending to roll Him down the hillside, but He slipped from their midst and disappeared, never again to return to that place where He had spent His whole young life.

These were His people, many of them His friends, and some may have always been hostile to Him for one reason or another. I am sure His friends felt bad, but what could they do against angry neighbors? They had to live with them. Rarely do friends have the courage to put themselves on the line when you face opposition or are going through a crisis. Then you are alone. They may secretly feel sorry for you, but it is empty comfort. Later the apostles would run away from Him at the most critical time of His life. It is the same with all of us. A time will come in each of our lives when we will be in difficult straits for one reason or other. At times like that you have to have the inner strength to go it alone, as very few friends have what it takes to stand by you when you face trouble, especially if it is over a public issue. Intimacy with Jesus, who will always be our friend when others walk away, is a special blessing, not to be taken lightly. Even when good things happen to us, and acclaim may come from far and wide, Jesus tells us, "Don't expect honor from those at home. It will not come." That will always be true. When a person accomplishes something great, he or she may be honored for it by strangers, but it is rare that family or neighbors are impressed. Even friends may not see anything remarkable in the person, and are still good friends.

With Jesus, however, some of the people from home were hostile to His mission of salvation. He could not help but feel bad about His family's neighbors turning against Him with such ferocity. His mother and her close relatives still had to live with all those people. It must have been particularly painful for her, but had not Simeon foretold that a sword would pierce her heart because of her Son's special mission?

Mary was beginning to see that Simeon's prophecy was coming true. And you wonder if some of those angry people would show up at the wedding party at Cana shortly after that incident. Cana was only a few miles away, and the people in both places were probably all acquainted with each other, if not related in some way.

It Is Not the Time My Father
Had Planned

*There was a marriage at Cana in Galilee, and the
mother of Jesus was there. Jesus also was invited to
the marriage, with his disciples. When the wine
failed, the mother of Jesus said to him, "They have
no wine." And Jesus said to her, "Woman, what
does that have to do with me? My hour has not yet
come." His mother said to the servants, "Do whatever he tells you." Now six stone jars were standing
there, for the Jewish rites of purification, each holding twenty or thirty gallons. Jesus said to them, "Fill
the jars with water." And they filled them up to the
brim. He said to them, "Now draw some out, and
take it to the steward of the feast." So they took it.
When the steward of the feast tasted the water now*

> become wine and did not know where it came from
> (though the servants who had drawn the water
> knew), the steward of the feast called the bride-
> groom and said to him, "Every man serves the good
> wine first, and when men have drunk freely, then
> the poor wine. But you have kept the good wine un-
> til now." This, the first of his signs, Jesus performed
> at Cana in Galilee, and manifested his glory, and
> his disciples believed in him. JN 2:1–11

THIS LITTLE EPISODE REVEALS SO MUCH ABOUT JE-
sus, and also about His mother. Cana was not far from
Nazareth. Probably many of the people living in Cana had
relatives and close friends in Nazareth. It is also possible
that the wedding party included relatives of Mary and Jesus. Mary and Jesus were invited. Jesus was away at the
time, but felt He should be there, even though He would
have to arrive late. Mary seems to have been very involved
with what was happening behind the scenes; she was the
one who noticed that the wine had run out. Think about
that for a moment. In those days, when a girl was born the
father would start that year to make an extra batch of
wine—one batch for his family and friends, and a second
batch in preparation for his daughter's wedding, some six-

teen years down the line. And perhaps the groom's father may have done something similar. This wedding party had been in progress for three days. During that time the guests had already finished the whole sixteen-year supply. You can imagine many things. It didn't seem to bother Mary that perhaps some of the guests may have been acting silly or getting too boisterous or not using good language. She was more concerned about the bride and groom being forever embarrassed over such a misfortune.

As soon as Jesus arrived, Mary went over to Him and dropped Him a hint: "Son, they've run out of wine." "So what, Mother, what do you expect me to do? My time has not yet come [that is, the time appointed by my Father]." Analyze that! Jesus scanned the scene and noticed the noisy atmosphere of the party. Some had had too much to drink. It didn't seem to bother Mary. Nor did it seem to bother Jesus. A Lebanese Christian once told me they still have those eight-day weddings back home in Lebanon, and he had very realistic memories of what it would have been like when Jesus arrived at that wedding party.

Think about Mary dropping Jesus a hint to do something, and Jesus took it as a hint, too. She must have seen Him doing tricks around the house. He didn't say no, and His mother did not take His answer as a refusal. She told the waiters to do whatever He told them. And look at what He did. He certainly was not stingy. Six stone water jars filled to the brim, 120 to 180 gallons, not just ordinary wine, but the best of wine, when the guests had already finished off a sixteen-year supply in only three days. And this was the premature inauguration day of Jesus' ministry as the Messiah. And look at how He introduced His ministry, not at the time His Father had planned, but because His mother asked Him, by giving a huge supply of good vintage wine to a poor family at their wedding party. Who says Mary is not a powerful intercessor with her Son?

And what are the messages? Certainly not that Jesus was encouraging people to drink too much. But this incident does show how comfortable God feels with His very human companions, at a party where some may have been a little too carefree. How uncritical and how beautiful is this God having fun at a party with His very human neighbors, and wanting them to have a good time! How many clergy would have done what Jesus did, under the circumstances, even if they did have the power to turn the water into wine?

It is interesting seeing Jesus being so human and so relaxed with His very human companions. We have a lot to learn about this God. Maybe we would be more accepting of our humanity if we understood how comfortable Jesus was with His humanity. I will never forget a picnic I attended with some friends. In the middle of the picnic a friend came up to me acting like a little kid. "What's got into you, Harry?" I said to him. "My father just told me he loved me. Father, you don't realize. That was the first time in my life he told me that he loved me." "How old are you, Harry?" "Seventy-five." "And how old is your father?" "Ninety-five, and he ain't even drunk, Father."

Can you imagine that man waited seventy-five years for his father to say he loved him, and when he did he started jumping around like a little kid? We are so afraid of being human, of showing tender feelings. God forbid anyone ever see us men cry! We are embarrassed at being human. And here we see Jesus having fun at a party and playing a big part in the celebration, and so casually overlooking the humanness of those at the party. If they knew that God was there, that would have put a damper on all the fun and ruined the party.

The message is clear. God wants us to enjoy our humanity—what we are, what He gave us. He did not make us perfect. He did not intend to. He gave us just what we need to do a little job, and all the rest of us is imperfect and defective. He knows that and accepts that in us. We may not like to be that way, and those who live with us may like it even less, but Jesus loves us as He made us, and He knows that in God's good time we will grow to be the way He plans for us to be, but only as He gives us the grace. So we do the best we can, and with humility ac-knowledge our weaknesses and struggle on. What is important to God is that we are sensitive to the pain and hurt in other people's lives and reach out to help them. The amazing thing about God is that He overlooks so many of our weaknesses. It is so obvious throughout the Gospels. Jesus is patient and though there are times when he feels frustrated with his apostles, like the time he rebuked Peter for his lack of faith ("Get behind me Satan! You are thinking not as God thinks, but as human beings do"), he rarely criticizes them. He shows the same patience to the crowds of sinners who follow him around Jerusalem. Jesus has compassion for these people, teaching them parables and healing the sick. It is also obvious that He rarely asks very much of any of us unless we are a specially chosen soul, and in those situations He drives us to accomplish what might ordinarily seem to be beyond mere human capability.

Want to Please God? Be a Child

*And Jesus called over a little child and had the
child stand in front of them, and said, "I warn you,
unless you become like this little child, you will not
enter the kingdom of heaven."* MT 18:2–3

WHAT IS THERE IN A LITTLE CHILD THAT WOULD
prompt Jesus to hold up that child as the model of
those allowed to enter heaven? Is it trust, simplicity, helplessness, vulnerability, innocence? The apostles were
proud of their macho outer shell. They enjoyed the prestige that went with being called as associates of Jesus.
These rough, uncouth fishermen were only too conscious
of their newfound importance in the company of this

highly refined and intelligent rabbi whose brilliance and holiness were unparalleled in all of Jewish society. That macho trait in the apostles troubled Jesus. He wanted them to learn that the traits they saw in the child were the traits He expected to see in them. The lesson was a shock to their egos, and though He spoke gently enough, His message deflated their air of self-importance. That air of conceit and pomposity He saw in the scribes, Pharisees, and chief priests that made them so obnoxious in the eyes of everyone—He was seeing this same trait developing in His apostles. He was worried that they might one day treat the disciples in the same manner that the religious leaders were treating the Jewish people. Arrogance was a trait foreign to Jesus. He still had the simplicity of a child and the innocence of a lamb, and He wanted to see those traits manifested in those who followed Him, especially in those who were to take His place in shepherding His disciples.

But Jesus' concern was not limited to the apostles. This is an admonition to all of us. Jesus is telling us what traits His Father would like to see in all of us if we want to enter into His kingdom. We must be like little children. What does that mean to us? What is it that Jesus is expecting of us? What is it that we can learn from a little child that can touch the heart of God and make us acceptable to Him?

When I am at Joshua House in Maryland I offer Mass

Want to Please God? Be a Child

And Jesus called over a little child and had the child stand in front of them, and said, "I warn you, unless you become like this little child, you will not enter the kingdom of heaven." MT 18:2–3

WHAT IS THERE IN A LITTLE CHILD THAT WOULD prompt Jesus to hold up that child as the model of those allowed to enter heaven? Is it trust, simplicity, helplessness, vulnerability, innocence? The apostles were proud of their macho outer shell. They enjoyed the prestige that went with being called as associates of Jesus. These rough, uncouth fishermen were only too conscious of their newfound importance in the company of this highly refined and intelligent rabbi whose brilliance and holiness were unparalleled in all of Jewish society. That macho trait in the apostles troubled Jesus. He wanted them to learn that the traits they saw in the child were the traits He expected to see in them. The lesson was a shock to their egos, and though He spoke gently enough, His message deflated their air of self-importance. That air of conceit and pomposity He saw in the scribes, Pharisees, and chief priests that made them so obnoxious in the eyes of everyone—He was seeing this same trait developing in His apostles. He was worried that they might one day treat the disciples in the same manner that the religious leaders were treating the Jewish people. Arrogance was a trait foreign to Jesus. He still had the simplicity of a child and the innocence of a lamb, and He wanted to see those traits manifested in those who followed Him, especially in those who were to take His place in shepherding His disciples.

But Jesus' concern was not limited to the apostles. This is an admonition to all of us. Jesus is telling us what traits His Father would like to see in all of us if we want to enter into His kingdom. We must be like little children. What does that mean to us? What is it that Jesus is expecting of us? What is it that we can learn from a little child that can touch the heart of God and make us acceptable to Him?

When I am at Joshua House in Maryland I offer Mass

at the local parish each Sunday. I know each of the little children and smile at them when I see them accompanying their parents for Communion. I take a moment, stoop down and talk to them, and bless them with the Host when I give Communion to their parents. At the back of the church after Mass they come to me and beam from ear to ear and give me a big hug. Even the boys do it. They are so trusting and so innocent. They have no air of self-consciousness. They are thrilled that someone has reached out to love them, and they respond by trusting this stranger in returning that love. It is so beautiful. I think that is the way God wishes we would love Him. But, unfortunately, He wishes in vain. We don't trust God enough to love Him with that kind of abandon. I think of that and I cannot help but feel for God and how it must hurt Him that we do not love Him that way.

But it is not just our lack of childlike love for God that hurts Him. Jesus is saying that in losing our childlikeness we lose something essential to our spiritual wholeness. We put a wall between ourselves and God. We say without words, "I don't trust you, God. So keep your distance. I will handle my own life. I don't trust you not to foul up my life and my plans." Even for those of us who trust God, there are limits to our trust. When we are in trouble or need we often don't trust Him enough to place ourselves in His loving care. We tell Him specifically what we would like Him to do for us, and what we expect of Him, but that is not the same as trusting Him. It is insulting. We are afraid that if we leave it up to Him, He may have ideas of His own, and that might not jibe with what we want. So we are very specific. Even when we pray, we keep Him at a distance.

How beautiful it would be if we, as big and important as we are, could be like the little children and run into His loving arms and say, "Father, I love you and trust you completely with my life. I am hurting and in trouble. I am frightened and alone without you, and I trust you completely to protect me and guide me." I think that is what Jesus was saying to the apostles, and to each of us.

Don't Embarrass God When You Pray

Now it happened that he was in a certain place praying, and when he had finished one of his disciples said, "Lord, teach us to pray, as John taught his disciples." LK 11:1

"When you pray, go into your room and shut the door and pray to your Father in secret, and your Father who sees what is secret will reward you. And in praying do not use many empty words like the pagans do, for they think they will be heard in their multiplicity of words. Do not be like them, for your Father knows what you need before you ask him. This is how you are to pray: Our Father, who are in heaven, hallowed be your name. Your kingdom come, your will be done on earth as it is in heaven.

*Give us this day our daily bread, and forgive us our
debts as we forgive our debtors. And lead us not into
temptation, but deliver us from evil. For if you forgive men their offenses, your heavenly Father will
forgive you. But if you do not forgive men their offenses, neither will your Father forgive your offenses."* MT 6:6–15

THIS IS AN INTERESTING SCENE, AND ANOTHER ONE
of those incidents that makes us stop and think. Jesus'
response is a shock. Today it is so common when religious people gather together, even at each other's homes,
to pause for a Bible reading or prayer. This practice has become so widespread you would think that that is what Jesus would do when He and the apostles paused during a
journey and were resting. Apparently Jesus did not gather
the apostles around Him for prayer or Bible reading. That
may come as a surprise to us, and it may have been something the apostles themselves could not understand, so
much so that one of them on this occasion asks Him why
He didn't pray with them the way John the Baptizer prayed
with his disciples and taught them how to pray.

I am reminded of a priest friend in Australia who
started a powerful movement to gather groups of people

together as friends all throughout Australia, and eventually in the United States. When the groups come together, they do not have prayers or Bible readings. The priest was severely criticized for this. His response was, "Did Jesus gather the apostles and His followers together and have prayers? He gathered people together to teach them how to care for one another and be there when someone needed them."

The scribes and Pharisees liked to be seen praying in public. This public display of their religiosity sickened Jesus, and He did not want anything like that to be part of His disciples' spirituality. "When you pray, go to your room and shut the door and pray to your Father in secret, and your Father who sees what is secret will reward you." On the surface it is shocking to hear Jesus say that, but when you think of it, conversation with God is a very private affair. Public worship by the community is a different thing. It is the community honoring God and offering gratitude as a family, and the public expression of our need for Him and for His help. That kind of prayer pleases God because we are gathering as His children to show Him our love and our gratitude, and to ask for His forgiveness.

Jesus was not opposed to praying to God in front of others. He did it Himself on a number of occasions, but there was always a reason for it, usually to give glory to His Father for some miracle that He was about to perform, for instance, when He was about to call Lazarus back to life. But ordinarily when Jesus prayed He went up into the hills and prayed alone, sometimes far into the night. There was an intimacy and privacy about His prayer. He needed to be alone with His Father to share with Him His experiences and His concerns about people's lack of faith and His inability to reach them, and to ask for strength and wisdom to do what had to be done.

At the Last Supper He prayed out loud. His prayer then was not only an intimate prayer with His Father; it was also His way of showing the apostles that now they were an intimate part of the divine family. And that prayer showed in a powerful way the sacred role they were to play in the divine plan of redemption. Jesus' prayer is beautiful and inspiring as He consecrated His apostles in His Father's love and commissioned them to continue His work of redemption throughout the world. Though it is too long to quote here, it is very worthwhile to read the whole prayer in the seventeenth chapter of Saint John's Gospel.

For Jesus prayer was an intimate act of love. People in love express that love privately. Even in Gethsemane when He brought the apostles with Him for human companionship and comfort He withdrew a distance from them when He entered into prayer with His Father. He wanted His apostles nearby but not intruding on the privacy and intimacy of His communing with His Father.

Our prayers should also be considered sacred and tender moments of intimacy with our Father, and with Jesus, and the Holy Spirit as well. There may be times when we may feel a need to pray with friends, but ordinarily it seems God wants to draw us into intimacy with Himself when we pray, so He can feel comfortable enough to share with us what we need, or the plans or insights He wants to reveal to us.

Why Did You Have to Wake Me?

When he got into a boat, his disciples followed him. Just then a powerful storm broke out on the sea, so that the boat was swamped by the waves, but he was asleep. So they came and woke him, and said to him, "Master, save us! We are going to drown!"

He said to them, "Why are you so afraid? Don't you have any trust in me?" Then he got up and rebuked the winds and the sea, and there was a great calm. MT 8:23–26

VIOLENT STORMS RUSH DOWN WITHOUT WARNING from Mount Hermon in Lebanon and wreak havoc on the Sea of Galilee. This was one of those storms that even these seasoned fishermen could not outmaneuver. They panicked. And Jesus was sound asleep in His shelter in the prow of the boat. What a picture!

Jesus must have been in a deep sleep. He must have been exhausted. I am sure He did not wake up full of joy. If He was human like us I can easily picture Him grumbling as He crawled out of His little shelter to see why they were so upset. Looking out at the weather that had disturbed His sleep He yelled out to the storm, "Calm down!" The storm stopped immediately and the wind and sea became calm. And grumbling over the apostles' lack of trust, He probably crawled back into His shelter to continue His sleep. If you were that tired wouldn't you have done the same?

Life is filled with these kinds of storms, maybe not storms of sea and waves but the many painful events that buffet us with unexpected force and leave us stunned. During an economic downturn, we may lose a job and not know what to do about mortgage payments, or children's college bills, or medical insurance. It could be an unexpected lawsuit is filed against us and we don't even have the money to retain a lawyer. Or it might be the horrible shock of a disastrous medical report or bad news about one of our children.

The first reaction is to panic. As humans we are so easily terrified, and, very much like the apostles, we don't know what to do. We plead, "Lord, save us. We are going to die," or something close to that. We don't know how we will ever survive this crisis. These situations happen to all of us at some time or other, and to some of us, frequently. After we get over the initial shock and ask God's help, we then begin to tell God what we would like Him to do. Unfortunately, this is not the way God works. If we deal with God this way we set ourselves up for disappointment. We want things to work out in a way that can make us feel comfortable; we want God to calm our panic. God has much longer term plans for us, understanding what is good for us. He will answer our prayers, in His time, but hardly ever in the way we might like.

The Chinese lady who did the painting for my little book *What Is God?* told me afterward that at the time she was working on the illustrations she was going through a very difficult crisis in her life that seemed to have no solution. As she finished each painting and continued on the others she noticed a strange calm coming over her, and when she finally finished the work the crisis had mysteriously vanished and she found herself at peace. She couldn't wait to tell me. What God eventually works out for us is sometimes hard for us to understand. We step aside and look at what He has done for us and can only say, "That's better than I ever dreamed—not what I wanted exactly, but much better."

The Publican with a Clean Heart

As Jesus was walking along the street in Capernaum, he caught sight of a man sitting in the tax collector's booth, a man named Matthew, and he said to him, "Come, follow me!" And he got up and followed him. MT 9:9

PICTURE THAT SCENE. JESUS WAS WALKING DOWN A busy street and notices Levi (whom we know as Matthew, the son of Alphaeus) in his tax collector's booth. I am sure Jesus knew Matthew would be there when He started out on His walk, just like He knew the Samaritan woman would be at the well when He decided to take the trip up to Samaria. Most probably Jesus had met Matthew before, or had seen him among the crowds that came to hear Him speak, and knew he was ready for the call. So when Jesus called him, Matthew was only too glad to give up his job, leave everything, and follow Jesus.

That day or shortly afterward Matthew threw a big retirement bash for himself and all his fellow tax collectors, and of course he invited Jesus and His closest friends. It must have been a loud, boisterous event, as the noise attracted Pharisees and their scribes to the source of the loud celebration. Looking through the large opening in the front of the banquet room, who did they see but a crowd of tax collectors and other so-called sinners? Naturally they were eating, drinking, making loud conversation, cracking jokes about each other and about the pompous and overbearing priests, and having a jolly good time. There may have even been hired musicians for entertainment. The center of attention at this happy party was none other than that new itinerant preacher, Jesus, that fellow who had been kicked out of Nazareth not long ago. And just like the rest of the sinners, they thought, He was having a great time for Himself. Look at Him! Some rabbi!

Not exactly the people's idea of the Messiah or even of a spiritual person, but that was Jesus. Jesus did not intend to conform to others' image of holiness. He was just Himself: happy, fun-loving, casual, enjoying being human, enjoying being with friends at a party, having a good time. It was an integral part of His idea of authentic holiness, loving life in its wholeness as His Father planned. He came to free people from the legal straitjackets the religious leaders had fashioned for them. "Come, follow me, and I will show you how to live. I am the way, the truth, and the light."

The tax collectors would never have had a party with the Pharisees. They were no fun. They were too holy. But, with God come down to earth, they felt right at home, and He with them. He demanded nothing of them, just their friendship. Their friendship with Him would in time change them; not necessarily their crusty manners, but they themselves would change completely from the inside out, their attitudes and values gradually improving, and in the process their external behavior changing as well.

It is the same with us. Jesus expects nothing of us but our friendship. It is His friendship that eventually changes us, without our even knowing it. Being His friend, living with Him in the intimacy of our meditations on His life in the Gospels and on what He means to us in our lives, we, like Matthew and the tax collectors and sinners, gradually follow in His way, as His light guides us and the warmth of His friendship comforts and strengthens us. With His love and His presence we need never fear.

Would You Hug a Leper?

When Jesus was in one of the towns, there was a man there covered with leprosy. Seeing Jesus he fell down with his face to the ground and begged him, "Sir, if you willed it, you could make me clean." Jesus reached out and touched him, and said to him, "I do will it. You are now clean." And the leprosy left him at once. Lк 5:12–13

LEPROSY IS A HIDEOUS DISEASE. IT WAS THE WORST thing that could happen to a person in Jesus' day, and even today it strikes fear and dread into people who witness it. In Jesus' day, it was considered a punishment from God for some evil committed. Once the disease was diagnosed, the person had to be cut off from the community, including family and loved ones. Often lepers gathered in isolated places and found shelter together in caves. Everyone avoided them. They often became hideous to look at as their flesh rotted away from the bones. Family might bring food and necessities and leave them where the leprous relative could find them. But contact was impossible, unless you were willing to go and live with them yourself. Touching them was forbidden. It was thought that if you touched a leper you could contract the disease.

This poor soul in the Gospel scene had lost all pride and feeling of self-worth. He fell to the ground and put his face in the dirt, honoring Jesus in a gesture of an abject, beaten human being. Jesus' heart went out to the fellow. Seeing the emptiness in the man's life and that he had not been touched by any human expression of love for a long time, Jesus reached out and touched him. It is very possible that Jesus may have really given him a hug and held him close as His healing power coursed through the man's body, making him whole again. This is again a symbol of Jesus embracing our pain. We are often repulsed by others' pain when tragic circumstances strike them. We don't know what to do or how to react, so we often shun the person, even if the person is close to us. We don't see Jesus acting that way. He is repulsed neither by our physical unsightliness nor by the hideousness of our sins. He feels compassion for whatever sorry state into which we have fallen, and He always reaches out to heal us. I will never forget the time that I went to see my godson Joey in a rehab center. When he approached me with a smile, happy to see me, all I could see was his pain. We hugged and I cried from so deep within me. "Why are you crying, Fahd?" "Because I feel your pain, Joe. Don't give up, Joe." "I won't, Fahd." And he didn't. He was eventually healed, and a short time later God took him home.

In that brief encounter I could understand Jesus' feelings for each of us. He feels our pain, and He wants to heal us. No matter how deeply we have fallen into sin and drifted away from God, it is not the evil we do that bothers Him or what our evil behavior does to Him. It is the pain that sin causes us that prompts Him to want to heal us. He said as much in telling us about the Good Shepherd. That is the mystery of God's love, which is so different from our response to hurt. When we are offended by someone we focus on how the person has hurt us. When we sin God feels the pain it causes us, and He doesn't give up until He can eventually heal us. It is only our unwillingness to let Him come close that prevents Him from healing us. But once we open our hearts to Him, the healing begins, even though the process may take time.

The Law Was Made for Man,
Not Man for the Law

On a particular Sabbath Jesus was walking through a field of grain. His disciples were picking the heads off the grain and rubbing them and then eating them. Some Pharisees said, "Why are you doing what is forbidden on the Sabbath?" Jesus said to them, "Have you not read what David did when he and his followers were hungry, how he went into the house of God and took the loaves of showbread, which only the priests were allowed to eat, and ate them and gave them to his followers to eat?" And he then said, "The Sabbath was made for man and not man for the Sabbath." MK 2:23–28

THIS SHORT PASSAGE IS FILLED WITH IMPORTANT issues. Understanding what is contained in this passage is the key to much of what Jesus is all about. To the religious leaders, Jesus and His disciples appeared to be arrogant in their apparent contempt for practices the Pharisees considered sacred, such as the Sabbath rest. Jesus and his disciples were casually walking around on the Sabbath, this time through a field of ripened grain. Interesting that the Pharisees were following them! The disciples broke a Sabbath law by picking grain and shelling it (harvesting grain on the Sabbath, as the Pharisees saw it), and then eating it.

The Pharisees complained about the violation. Jesus shocked them further by citing an incident they would certainly have considered sacrilegious: David's taking the sacred loaves from the holiest room in the house of God and giving the bread to his followers because they were hungry. The showbread, as it was called, symbolized the living presence of God among the people, prefiguring the Eucharist, the real living presence of Jesus reserved in the tabernacles in our churches. We would be horrified if we saw someone break open the tabernacle and start eating the Eucharist for lunch, even if the person was desperately hungry. The Pharisees probably had the same reaction to what David did. Jesus refreshed the Pharisees' memory of that event and held it up to them for their consideration.

They wouldn't dare criticize David, the "man after God's own heart" and the legendary national hero. Then Jesus said two shocking things; only one is mentioned in the quote cited at the beginning of this chapter. He said, "The Son of man is Lord of the Sabbath," and then He stated the Lord's official purpose of the Sabbath: "The Sabbath was made for man and not man for the Sabbath."

In reading that statement over and over it finally dawned on me that Jesus had a lot of issues concerning the Sabbath bottled up inside Him. This was a good occasion to get much of that stuff out of His system. His remark about the purpose of the Sabbath shocked me, so I asked a rabbi friend what was the original reason for God's commanding the Sabbath rest. His reply was, to protect slaves from their masters' working them to death. They, and not only they but everybody, had to observe the Sabbath as a day of rest, a day to relax and have fun, and get the family together and enjoy themselves. In that God found delight. To Him that time was the people's prayer of praise and joy. As time went on the religious leaders didn't feel comfortable with people having such a good time on the day of rest, so they began making endless laws until they ended up outlawing hundreds of activities on the Sabbath, making enjoyment of the day impossible.

The mean-spirited hypocrisy of these laws saddened Jesus because the laws destroyed the special time His

Father had set aside for His people. The Pharisees, if they were really well-versed in the history of the Sabbath, would have known that Jesus was right. Jesus went a step further and raised the issue of an even more important law, concern for the needs of God's children, for which the Pharisees had little sympathy. David took the sacred loaves from the Holy Place because there was a human need. Of primary concern to Jesus were the anguish and needs of His Father's children who had been so cruelly treated by religious leaders for centuries. He was relentless in pointing this out to the religious leaders whenever they brought up infringements to those meaningless and mean-spirited prohibitions.

The Pagan Soldier with a Humble Heart

A servant of a certain centurion was dying. He was dear to the centurion, who upon hearing of Jesus sent Jewish elders to him asking him to come and save his servant. When they came to Jesus they entreated him earnestly, saying to him, "He is worthy that you should do this for him, for he loves our nation and he has built our synagogue for us."

So Jesus went with them, and when he was not far from the house, the centurion sent friends to say to him, "Lord, do not trouble yourself. I am not worthy that you should come under my roof. This is why I did not think myself worthy to come to you. But say the word and my servant will be healed. For I too am a man subject to authority, and have men subject to me; and I say to one, 'Come' and he comes and to another, 'Do this,' and he does it."

> *When Jesus heard this he marveled, and turn-*
> *ing to the crowd that followed him, said, "In truth,*
> *I have not found such great faith even in Israel."*
> *And when the messengers returned to the house*
> *they found the servant who had been ill healed.*
> LK 7:2–9

THERE IS A REMARKABLE ELEMENT IN THIS STORY that, after all my years of study, I just began to realize. In so many of the other miracles Jesus performed there was a remarkable manifestation of faith and trust in each of the people who asked Jesus for healing, except for Mary and Martha, who seemed to believe that Jesus could not help them once their brother was dead. "You're too late. Why didn't you come earlier?"

In this incident the outstanding difference is in the depth of the centurion's faith. He had such a respect for Jesus that he felt he was unworthy to approach Him, so he sent Jewish elders as emissaries to intercede for him. And even as Jesus was approaching the centurion's house, intending to enter, the centurion did not consider himself worthy that Jesus should show him such honor, so he sent out friends to tell Jesus that he was not worthy enough for Jesus to grace his house with His presence.

Jesus was truly amazed. What is so stunning here is the

quality of this man's faith and trust. It is a faith that is enhanced by a delicate humility. Jesus had never seen that kind of faith before. The vast majority of the other requests for healing were made by direct appeal to Jesus. The people approached Him and bluntly, if imploringly, begged Him to heal them. In the only other incident involving humility a father whose son was dying did not want Jesus to trouble Himself by traveling all the way to his house to cure his son. Just Jesus' willing that the son be healed was all that was necessary.

A reason, perhaps, why the centurion was hesitant about Jesus entering his house was that he was aware that it was forbidden for a Jew to enter the house of a pagan, and the Jew would incur legal uncleanness if he did so. The centurion certainly did not want this holy man to be considered contaminated in the eyes of His own people. And Jesus clearly appreciated the delicacy of this foreigner's sensitivity, and was overwhelmed by the man's thoughtfulness.

But there is another reason that Jesus was so impressed with this man's faith, and that is the real message for us in this story. There are many Christians who say we should go directly to Jesus with our prayer requests. Most people in the Gospels confronted Jesus personally when they needed healing. But Jesus was touched by the humble delicacy of this man, because he felt the need to ask someone more worthy than himself to approach Jesus for a healing.

Jesus' response is stunning: "I have never seen such faith even in all of Israel."

And the way we pray is rather confusing. We ask others to pray for us and intercede when we need divine help, but then some of us say that we should not use heavenly intercessors with Jesus but should go to Him directly. And we use that reasoning when it comes to those most close to God in heaven. If we feel comfortable asking for our friends' intercession, why should we be shy about asking our deceased mothers and fathers and other saintly friends, especially Jesus' Mother in heaven, to intercede for us? The dichotomy does not make sense. We say in the Apostles' Creed, "I believe in the communion of saints," that mystical intimate bonding that exists between ourselves and our loved ones and special sainted friends who are continually in God's presence. Those bonds of love are real, and we can be sure that if we have a saintly mother or father in heaven, he or she is certainly going to be pestering God on our behalf. Our friends in heaven, especially those who have personalities and difficulties like our own, would be only too willing to act on their love for us by talking to God on our behalf. Wouldn't you if you were a saint in God's presence and a poor sinner was begging for your prayers?

The message in this incident with the centurion is his humility as well as his certain faith that Jesus could do something to help his servant.

When We Condemn, We Are Condemned

At daybreak Jesus again came into the temple, and all the people came to him; and sitting down he began to teach them.

Now the scribes and Pharisees brought a woman caught in adultery, and setting her in the midst said to him, "Master, this woman has just been caught in adultery. And in the Law Moses commanded us to stone such persons. What do you say?" Now they were saying this to test him, that they might be able to accuse him. But Jesus, stooping down, began to write with his finger on the ground.

When they continued asking him, he stood up and said to them, "Let him who is without sin be the first to cast a stone at her." And again stooping down, he began to write on the ground. But hearing

> *this, they went away, one by one, beginning with the eldest. And Jesus remained alone, with the woman standing in the midst.*
>
> *Jesus stood up and said to her, "Has no one condemned you?" "No one, Lord." Then Jesus said, "Neither will I condemn you. Be on your way and avoid this sin."* JN 8:2–11

H<small>OW DO YOU FIND A PERSON COMMITTING ADUL-</small>tery, and early in the morning? This is interesting. These sanctimonious legalists must have been snoops. Were they going around peeking in people's windows? Did they have spies? And why was it that they could only find the woman? Whatever. When they finally arrived at Jesus' group of followers and threw the woman down at His feet, He was disgusted with their hypocrisy. He ignored them and started scratching something in the dirt. When they persisted, He said to them, "All right, if that's the Law, then stone her, but let him who is without sin among you cast the first stone." One of the early Fathers of the Church said that what Jesus was writing in the dirt were the secret sins of each of the scribes and Pharisees. And when they saw their dirty private lives about to be revealed they dropped their stones and slinked away.

Again, sin is an affront to God, but for some strange reason it is not God but humans who delight in punishing sinners. What Jesus sees in sinners is their pain and what leads them into sin. He never condones people's sins, but neither does He have an obsession to punish people for their sins. In this incident, he didn't take the side of the woman, but He made it very clear that if you are going to be the judge of other people's sins, you had better be innocent yourself. The self-righteous legalists were always contemptible to Jesus. Their hypocrisy sickened Him, and He always spoke out against it whenever they confronted Him. They were people devoid of love and compassion. They had no feeling for people's pain and their anguished lives.

You see this mentality more and more in society, the self-righteous need of some people to see sinners punished to the fullest extent of the law. "Let them rot in jail," "Execute them," "Protect society, and eliminate them from our midst." Politicians pride themselves on demanding more severe sentences for crimes than their opponent. This mentality of demanding ever more severe punishments for crime will cry to heaven for vengeance. At this rate society will revert to the days when you could be sentenced to prison for years for stealing a loaf of bread. A change has already begun to take place. In one instance a former prison inmate was released from prison, and, having no one to go home to, after a few days of freedom he stole some food because he was so hungry. He was immediately charged, arrested, and sent to prison for years. Pontius Pilate will never die. He appears so often in self-righteous societies and in politically driven judges and district attorneys who sacrifice human lives and reputations for votes. The reason that Jesus had such a difficult time with the scribes and Pharisees was that they could not see the great evil of which they were guilty—their sin was hideous compared to the sins they gleefully exposed and condemned in others. Their sin was choosing not to love or show compassion, while remaining blind to their own sins. Their whole life was lived out in denial of all that God is, LOVE. They were God's chosen teachers, the magisterium in Yahweh's religion, and their lives taught the opposite of God's very nature. The scribes and Pharisees felt it their duty to invent endless laws to protect their religion, and to punish sinners who violated those laws. It is strange, but God does not have a need to punish or destroy sinners. As the Good Shepherd He searches out those driven away by the Pharisees of every age and tries to bring them back home. He never gives up prodding even the worst of us sinners to change our hearts and turn back to His love. Our society is often only too willing to snatch sinners away from the Shepherd and execute them so He can have no further chance to save them. And the news media are probably responsible for destroying more souls and families than even unjust and dishonest prosecutors, judges, and immoral investigators who trick often innocent and frightened suspects into untruthful confessions and pleas. Jesus warns all of us that we will be judged at the Last Judgment with the same justice and mercy we dish out to others. We will be answerable mostly for the lives we have destroyed, the souls we have driven away from God. Some among the religious and public officials charged with the responsibility to be just and merciful have the most to fear from God.

We Judge by What We See on the Outside; He Judges by What He Sees in Our Hearts

One of the Pharisees invited Jesus to dinner. Jesus went into the Pharisee's house and reclined at table. To everyone's surprise a woman known in the town as a sinner, on hearing that he was at table in the Pharisee's house, brought an alabaster jar of ointment. Standing behind him at his feet, she began to bathe his feet with her tears and wipe them with her hair, and kissed his feet and anointed them with ointment.

When the Pharisee who had invited him saw this, he said to himself, "This man, if he were a prophet, he would certainly know who and what kind of a woman this is who is touching him, that she is a sinner."

Jesus answered and said to him, "Simon, I have something to say to you." And he said, "Master, say it." "A certain moneylender had two debtors. One owed him five hundred denarii, the other owed him fifty. As they had no way to pay, he forgave them both. Which one would love him the more?" Simon said in reply, "He, I imagine, to whom he forgave more." And he said to him, "You have judged correctly."

Turning to the woman, he said to Simon, "Do you see this woman? I came into your house, and you gave me no water for my feet, but this woman has not ceased to wash my feet with her tears and wipe them with her hair. You gave me no kiss, but from the moment she came in, she has not ceased to kiss my feet. You did not anoint my head with oil, but she has anointed my feet with ointment. So I say to you, her sins, as many as they may be, are forgiven her, because she has loved much. But he to whom little is forgiven loves little." And he said to her, "Your sins are forgiven." And those at table with him began to say to themselves, "Who is this man, who even forgives sins?" He then said to the woman, "Your faith has saved you. Go in peace." Lᴋ 7:36–50

THIS TOUCHING SCENE IS FILLED WITH MESSAGES, some of which have never been developed. It is interesting that a leading Pharisee would invite Jesus to dinner. It seems that the Pharisees sensed Jesus had no bad feelings against Pharisees although publicly they disputed over the Law. This Pharisee felt comfortable inviting Jesus to his house for dinner, knowing that Jesus never held grudges and never passed up an occasion to discuss honestly matters of God's interest.

Rumor spread fast that Jesus was at Simon's house for dinner. What a topic for gossip! Hearing this, a woman who is referred to as a sinner immediately went home, picked up a jar of costly ointment, and ran down to the Pharisee's house. Barging in, she went over to Jesus, fell down at His feet, and started to cry uncontrollably, the tears so copious that they bathed His feet.

The Gospel does not say that the woman was a prostitute, but she was known to be a sinner, which most probably meant she was a prostitute or a woman of loose morals. She was clearly a woman of strong emotions, and a free spirit, not at all afraid of crashing the party of these revered officials to show her feelings for Jesus.

Whatever kind of sinner she was, Jesus was not the slightest bit embarrassed at her display of such affection for Him. But the Pharisee's mind was working feverishly, wondering how these two knew each other, and where this wild display of love for this wandering preacher had come from. How did He know *her?*

According to the Jewish social customs of the time, a man was not to talk to a woman in public, and he was certainly not to touch a woman, or allow a woman to touch him, especially a sinful woman. A man and a woman who were not married would never touch each other in public, or even talk to each other. Even in synagogues, men and women had to be separated. For this woman to be so free in showing affection to Jesus, crying so copiously that her tears bathed His feet, and holding His feet and drying them with her hair, and kissing His feet, had to be shocking. Such intimacy!

Imagine being in a crowded restaurant with your family and friends, and a well-known prostitute comes into the restaurant and spots you, then comes over and makes a big fuss over you! How would you feel? Jesus was at dinner with all the clergy in town, and He was not the slightest bit embarrassed. How beautiful! What an incredible God! So comfortable with a notorious sinner!

What was it about Jesus that touched that woman's heart so deeply? What was there between these two that she could be so intimate with Him? Had she heard Him speak and had she been healed of some terrible ache in her soul, or was she touched so profoundly by something that Jesus said that it changed her whole life? He must have healed her in some way, because she took advantage of an opportunity to show her gratitude. Perhaps she was passing by the Pharisee's house and noticed how the host had snubbed Jesus when He entered, after greeting all the other guests so warmly.

When Jesus spoke to Simon, He was genteel enough. He talked about a wealthy man, obviously God the Father, who loaned out huge sums of money to two people. To one he loaned a million dollars. To the other he loaned five hundred. Neither could pay him back, so he forgave both of them. Which one would love him more? The one he forgave the more, the Pharisee told Jesus. Jesus agreed, but He went further and introduced a shocking answer. This woman's huge debt was forgiven not only because of the goodness of the debtor but also because God saw goodness in her. The huge debt of her many sins was forgiven because "she loved much." God knew she was a sinner, but He also saw that in secrecy the woman cared for others in need; perhaps she fed and clothed orphans, old people, and widows who had no one to care for them. God saw the good she did, which no one in the community was even aware of, and this loving care of others in need preserved intact the bond of love between her and God. She was still in God's love and friendship in spite of her sins. The hint is also made that Simon's debt, though small, presented a difficulty for God because Simon had never learned to love or feel other people's pain.

Now that is an interesting theological twist that has not been well developed. We were all taught, no matter what religion or denomination we belong to, that committing a mortal sin destroys our relationship with God and cuts us off from Him, by destroying that bond of love with God. But that is not what Jesus is saying here. Here is a million-dollar sinner and Jesus said that as bad as her sins were she was still in God's friendship because of her love and care for others.

This incident immediately brings to mind Jesus' relationship with Peter. I don't think we will ever love Jesus the way Peter loved Jesus, yet until the day we die we hope we will never commit the kind of sin that Peter committed, denying three times that he ever knew Jesus, and only an hour after he had made his first communion at the Last Supper. And you may ask yourself, "Were they still friends?" Of course they were still friends. Peter still loved Jesus more than the rest, and Jesus' love for Peter never diminished. Only now Jesus knew that He had a coward for a friend. So what else is new? And it was not long after that Jesus confronted Peter and, still smarting from Peter's denial, asked him three times, "Do you really love me, Peter?"

It is the same with us. We try to do what is right, yet we fail miserably. God knows we mean well, and He also knows that we are frightfully weak. He seems to take that for granted, and also that even with our best efforts we still fail. Jesus shows in this episode at the Pharisee's house that what concerns Him is our love and care for others. Are we sensitive to others and do we try to reach out to those in need? That is what Jesus saw in this woman who was despised by the townsfolk as a sinner; that is what prompted Him to say that because of her love for others her sins were forgiven. We don't stress that teaching of Jesus. If we did we could bring a lot of healing to people who almost despair of God's forgiveness. If God sees that caring love in us we can be sure He will say to us the same thing He said about the woman—that she was saved because she "loved much." And if we follow her example, after we die we will hear those beautiful words, "Come blessed of my Father into the kingdom prepared for you from the beginning of time." "When I was hungry, you gave me food; when I was thirsty, you gave me drink, [and so forth]. As long as you did it to the least of my brethren you did it to me."

When You Pray, Pray to Your Father in Secret

And long before dawn, Jesus retired up to a deserted place to pray. MT 14:23 AND MK 1:35

HOW MANY TIMES THE GOSPELS MENTION JESUS going up the mountain to spend the night in prayer! What a beautiful picture! The apostles go home to their families, and Jesus goes up into the hills to pray. Far away from everyone, totally alone, He fell down on His knees, sat back on His heels, rested His hands in His lap, closed His eyes, and immediately found Himself in the presence of His Father. Everything around Him faded from His sight. He was in another dimension, His Father's world.

One could imagine Jesus sharing with His Father His daily experiences. "Father, I am so glad to be with you tonight. You are my only comfort. I love my friends, especially those I have chosen, but I feel so alone with them because they cannot understand, nor do I expect them to. I reach out to them and they look at me without understanding. Only you understand, Father, and I am grateful for your closeness to me. You are always with me. You are my strength, my comfort, my joy.

"When I first began to speak to the people, they came and listened. I was new. They were curious, especially when I healed their sick and their crippled. Then they began to come in vast crowds, for healing rather than to learn. When I preached to them they were impressed and went and told their friends. The crowds grew to even greater numbers. But now they are beginning to change, Father. I can tell. When I talked of the kingdom, they saw a messianic kingdom conquering other kingdoms. When I talked about storing up treasures, they thought of gold and silver and material treasures. When they realized I was not interested in a worldly kingdom, or in gold and silver, but that my real interest was in your kingdom, Father, the kingdom of heaven, their interest fast began to cool. Things are changing, Father. The scribes and Pharisees, who have your authority to teach, have become my enemies. Their hatred is frightening. I see them and their spies in the crowds that follow me. They jot down notes to report me to the priests. Lately they have teamed up with the Sadducees, and even with the Herodians. They all hate each other. But in their hatred of me, Father, they have found a common ground. I am frightened, but not for myself. They can do nothing to touch me unless I choose, but they close in on me with such insistence that they make my mission difficult to carry out. I have to admit, Father, I am concerned, and I am becoming discouraged. I have tried so hard. There were so many things I wanted to accomplish for you, but I am fast finding that it is beyond me. I never realized how much free will can complicate my mission. When I expect these people to understand what I'm doing and cooperate with me, they as often frustrate my plans.

"Father, recently I offered the people myself as the food of their souls. They said I was ridiculous. They should have listened to me and accepted what I said. I had multiplied the loaves and fishes to feed them the night before, and they were impressed. But when I offered them my flesh and blood as the food of their souls, they laughed at me and then walked away. Even Judas began to change at that moment. I could tell.

"Father, I feel so sad. I cannot help but think that I have failed. Oh, I know I have not failed in what I came to accomplish, to give my life for the salvation of the world, but there were so many other things I wanted to accomplish for you, Father. I wanted to gather all your people together into your family and present them to you, but they do not accept what I offer to them. Father, I am so tired. Each day is tiring now, as I give all I have, and they do not respond. The apostles, they mean well, but they are so slow to understand. Most of the time they cannot understand even the simplest things I teach them. I know they mean well, and I really cannot fault them, but I feel I give all I can and there is so little response, so little understanding. Father, I am so tired, so tired."

Then, I think of Jesus, totally exhausted from this intensive kind of prayer, falling down on the ground, wrapping His cloak around Him, resting His head against the root of a tree, and going off into a deep sleep. I think that is the way Jesus must have prayed, laying bare His soul to His Father and drawing from Him the strength and comfort He so badly needed.

It Is Our Sins That Entitle Us to His Mercy

Publicans and sinners were crowding around Jesus to listen to him. Pharisees and scribes were murmuring, "This man welcomes sinners and eats with them."

He responded with this parable: "What man among you having a hundred sheep and losing one of them does not leave the ninety-nine in a deserted place and go after the one that was lost until he finds it? And when he has found it, he lays it on his shoulders rejoicing. And on coming home he calls together his friends and neighbors, telling them, 'Rejoice with me because I have found my sheep that was lost.' I tell you, there will be more joy in heaven over one sinner who repents than

> *over ninety-nine just who have no need of repentance."* Lk 15:1–7

SEE HOW JESUS GIVES US THESE BEAUTIFUL INsights into the heart of God. When He talks about sinners, He seems to be the one who is vulnerable and worried, like a shepherd who can't find one of his sheep and is nervous until he tracks it down and finds it. Then he is so happy at finding it, he places it on his shoulders and *carries* the sheep back home. And He extends the joy even further, saying that even in heaven there is great rejoicing when a lost sheep is saved. What kind of a God is this who worries about just one lost sheep? This is the same God who feels sorry for a crowd chasing after Him because they seem "like sheep without a shepherd."

We are the sheep. We are lost not because we are wandering aimlessly in a geographical sense. We are lost because we are sinners. We have done wrong. We have hurt others. We have used others. We have turned our backs on others, sometimes even loved ones, when it is for our convenience. We are lost because we have been selfish and have done evil things. We are thieves and bandits, and adulterers and cheats and murderers, and pedophiles, and sex offenders of all types, and decent people who out of weakness fall into sin. We are the ones who are judged by society as misfits, often judged justly, but very often the victims of unjust judges, and cops who trap innocent people into committing felonies, and district attorneys, who over-indict to frighten innocent people into plea-bargaining, and agreeing to crimes they never committed. We are the sinners who fall victim to heartless clergy who, like scribes and Pharisees, drive the sheep into the desert where they become lost and, wandering aimlessly, lose hope.

We are the sinners whom the righteous and self-righteous detest. They scream for our conviction, our imprisonment, and our execution. Were our judgment left up to them we would never have hope of forgiveness or redemption. But, fortunately, this strange God has not abandoned our eternal destiny into the hands of the righteous and self-righteous. He reserves that to Himself because He loves us and worries about us and is continuously searching for us no matter what we have done, or how bad we have been or in what godforsaken places we find holes to hide in or in whatever masquerades we camouflage our sinfulness to escape detection. Like the "Hound of Heaven," He tracks us down and, pitying our condition, picks us up and holds us to His heart as He carries us back home where He can care for us and heal us. And even when we are rotting in prison cells or solitary confinement, or waiting for our execution, He is there with us continually touching our souls with His grace until we finally relent and turn to Him and allow Him to redeem and save us. In the Gospels it was not the sinners He had problems with; it was the self-righteous who made Him sick to His stomach because they were without love or compassion and their lives were the living denial of everything that God is—love and compassion. They are the ones who have to worry about the judgment of God because of the unfeeling meanness they have shown toward the desperate and hopeless.

The Excommunicated Holy Man

"Who is my neighbor?" the lawyer asked Jesus. Jesus replied, "A man was going down from Jerusalem to Jericho and he encountered robbers who stripped him and beat him and left him lying half dead. Now a priest happened to be going down that road. When he saw him, he passed by on the other side of the road. Then a Levite likewise passed that way. He saw him and passed by on the other side. But a Samaritan as he journeyed came to where he was. When he saw him he had compassion and went to him and bound up his wounds, pouring on oil and wine, then set him on his own beast and brought him to an inn and took care of him. The next day he took out two denarii and gave them to the innkeeper, telling him, 'Take care of him, and

> *whatever more you spend, I will repay you on my way back.' Which of these three do you think showed himself a neighbor to the man who fell among the robbers?" And he said, "The one who showed him mercy." "Go and do likewise," Jesus said.* LK 10:29–37

HOW FAMILIAR JESUS MUST HAVE BEEN WITH THE dusty, dangerous trail down the steep hill from Jerusalem to Jericho. It had always been a barren land, and a danger to lone travelers because of the bands of robbers lurking along the way. On this particular occasion a lone traveler was waylaid and left lying half dead along the roadside. How many passed by Jesus does not mention, though it was left up to the listeners to examine their own consciences to ask themselves what they would have done in similar circumstances. Jesus singles out a priest and a Levite. Even though they were His Father's religious officials, He never hesitated to single them out for failing to care for the hurting sheep in His Father's flock. Caring for others was their duty.

On this occasion the wounded sheep was a wretched victim of assault and robbery. He must have been badly beaten because he was lying by the roadside, half dead. A priest going down the road saw him lying there, looked at him, saw blood all over the fellow, and not willing to incur contamination by touching blood, walked to the other side of the road and continued on his way. It was none of his business. Why should he bother? So he left the fellow there to die. Not long after, a Levite, another priest of lower rank, happened to come down that road. He too saw the poor wretch. Seeing the bloody mess lying there, and unwilling to be contaminated, he, too, walked to the other side of the road and continued on his way. It was none of his business. He, too, left the fellow there to die. How callous! But that seems to be what Jesus thought of the priests of His day.

I wondered whether this was just a parable, or if Jesus was relating an experience He had had one day on His way down that dangerous road. Had He acted like the Good Samaritan on that occasion? That was a thought that crossed my mind as I recently reread the parable. The parable reveals how perfectly Jesus sized up a common attitude among people even today. We don't like to get involved in other people's problems. There are too many possibilities for legal entanglements and so many unknowns that can complicate our lives. Even being a witness to an accident can tie up our lives in ways we could not foresee. Seeing a person drowning, about to be hit by a car, or in imminent danger of serious harm presents for us a problem demanding a decision. What do we do? Do we jump into the water and try to save the person? Do we run out and pull the person away from the path of a speeding car? Do we put our own lives in jeopardy to save someone else? "Greater love than this no one has than that he lay down his life for another," Jesus once remarked.

Practically every day an occasion arises for each of us to help someone, mostly in small ways, but occasionally in a situation that is significant. It is not always easy to make a decision even over a small matter. "Don't get involved!" is a popular bit of advice today.

The Good Samaritan in Jesus' parable did become involved. His own trip was delayed, possibly by another day. He had to take time out to care for the poor wretch, whom he did not even know, except that he seemed to be a Jew. For a Samaritan, helping a Jew would be a difficult decision. He put the man on his own donkey, while he himself had to walk the distance to the nearby khan for shelter. While there he cared for him overnight, and then he paid the khan attendant out of his own pocket. After instructing the attendant to care for the wounded man, he promised to pay any extra expenses on his way back. This was no insignificant involvement, and for a person he did not even know.

After relating that parable, Jesus asked the lawyer, "Who showed himself neighbor to the wounded man?" The lawyer could not get himself to even mouth the word "Samaritan," but merely said, "The one who showed him compassion." And Jesus said, "You have answered rightly. Go and do likewise."

Who Will Be Invited to Live in God's Home?

"There was a rich man who used to clothe himself in the latest styles and who feasted every day with splendid banquets. And outside at the gate of the rich man's estate lay a poor wretch named Lazarus, rotting away from disease and longing for some crumbs that fell from the rich man's table. Even the dogs used to come and lick his sores. Finally the poor man died and was carried away by angels to Abraham's family in heaven. The rich man also died and was buried in hell. Lifting up his eyes, being in torment, he saw Abraham afar off and the poor man in his presence, and he cried out, 'Father Abraham, have pity on me, and send Lazarus to dip the tip of his finger in water and cool my tongue, for I am in torment in this flame.'

"But Abraham said to him, 'Son, remember that you in your lifetime had received good things, and Lazarus likewise received evil things, but now he is here comforted and you in torment. Besides, there is a great void between you and us, so that those who wish to pass from here to there cannot, nor can anyone pass from your side to here.'

"And he said, 'Then, father, I beg you to send him to my father's house, for I have five brothers, that he may testify to them, lest they end up in this place of torments.' And Abraham said to him, 'They have Moses and the prophets, let them take heed of them.' But he said, 'No, father Abraham, if someone goes to them from the grave, they will believe, and repent.' And Abraham replied, 'If they do not believe Moses and the prophets, they will not believe even if someone comes back from the dead.'"

Lk 16:19–31

To MANY PEOPLE TODAY, THIS PARABLE OF JESUS IS pure fantasy, because they don't believe in heaven or hell. If cynics accept this material world as real, then why do they have such a hard time believing in a world Jesus tells us about? He should know. He is the Creator of both.

Why would He lie about the existence of other worlds? As a priest I have had access to so many stories about people's experiences that are far outside the natural. Some of these stories are without any credibility, but there are some that even the most cynical and skeptical would find hard to throw off as unbelievable. The stories of things that happened after the death of my godson are the most vivid. The morning after Joey had died his father told the family that Joey had appeared to him the night before. The family thought he was cracking up, and Joey's brother John came to work later that morning and told me I should talk to his father because he was having hallucinations.

I did talk to his father, and he told me what had happened. When he went to bed, the room was dark, and hovering over the foot of the bed was a ball of light with the edges shimmering. It seemed to be a self-contained energy force. It made him so peaceful, he fell to sleep immediately. When he woke up at three o'clock it was still there, and the same at five-thirty, when he had to get up and get ready for work. This happened many times. John had the same experience later, and that experience lasted for two and a half hours. When he found he could communicate with the object and it responded, though not verbally, when John talked about the things they used to do as kids, then John knew it was his brother making his presence known. John said he would never again doubt the existence of life after death. The evening after Joey had been buried, his uncle, a very unemotional engineer, asked me if there had been any electric lights near Joey's grave. When I told him no, he was surprised and then told me that when he had gotten up in the middle of the night to go to the bathroom he had seen a bright ball of light hovering over Joey's grave.

In this parable Jesus gives us a further insight into God's mind. He is not critical of the rich man for being rich, or for dressing well and eating well. He criticizes him for his callous heartlessness toward the poor leper dying of starvation right at his doorstep. God is not even talking about violations of the Ten Commandments; He is concerned only about the rich man's insensitivity to the misery of the poor starving leper.

Jesus doesn't even say that *God* sent the rich man to hell. It is as if we choose our place after death by the way we live. If we have cut God and other people out of our lives, and live only for ourselves, never learning how to love or even caring to love, whether God or our fellow human beings in need, then our lives after death are a logical extension of our lives on earth. We go to a place where God cannot intrude, and we meet up with all the other people like ourselves who are totally devoid of love or caring for anyone but themselves, who are incapable of reaching out to anyone else. Imagine living forever with people who are totally in love with themselves, with no one ever caring for you or capable of loving you!

Heaven has to be the same logical extension of our lives here on earth. People who have centered their lives on God and have cared for their fellow human beings in need will logically find themselves, after they pass through the veil of death, in a life that is still centered on God and the companionship of all the good caring beings whose eternal existence is filled with love and ecstatically bonded to God's love.

Moses and Elijah Surprise the Apostles

Jesus took with him Peter, James, and John and led them up a high mountain where they could be by themselves. Then in their presence he was transfigured. His clothes became dazzlingly white, whiter than any fuller could make them. Elijah and Moses appeared to them, and they were speaking with Jesus. Then Peter said to them, "Rabbi, it is good for us to be here. Let us build three shelters, one for you, one for Moses, and one for Elijah." He did not know what he was saying, they were all so frightened. Then a cloud appeared, covering them, and a voice came from the cloud saying, "This is my beloved Son. Listen to him." Then suddenly they looked around and saw no one, only Jesus.

Then as they were coming down the mountain,

he warned them to tell no one of the vision until the
Son of Man has risen from the dead. Mk 9:2–9

IT IS SO DIFFICULT FOR ME TO COMMENT ON THIS part of the Gospel. It reveals so much of Jesus' inner life and the heavy, painful thoughts weighing down so mightily upon Him. He knew only too vividly that His last days were nearly upon Him. Images of betrayal and torture and horrible death were flooding His mind with nightmares even during the day. He spent more and more quiet time with His Father, the only one who could give Him strength to face what was about to happen in Jerusalem. It is all so vivid. His divine mind saw with such graphic clarity; it was too much for His human spirit to struggle with all at once. He was frightened—it is not that He was afraid of dying; He came down to earth for that. But He was afraid of all that His death would entail: His people turning against Him; the terrible tortures that would be inflicted; the false accusations and trials before His Father's own chosen teachers and priests, whose spiritual emptiness He has tried so hard to fill with light and love; the shame and humiliation He would have to suffer before His own creatures; the cowardice of His best friends, His chosen apostles, who would run from Him; Peter's denying three times that he ever knew Him; and the horrible torment of the Crucifixion. All these things filled His soul with dread.

On this occasion He brought with Him Peter, James, and John. They needed to be there. They needed to glimpse something of His glory. They needed to be impressed by seeing Moses, the great lawgiver, and Elijah, the fiery prophet, meet intimately with their Lord, evidencing for the three apostles that Jesus was the fulfillment of the Law and the prophecies. It is so obvious that Jesus was going through a serious crisis and in His struggle was trying to prepare His closest friends for the worst. Seeing Jesus so vulnerable, I find it hard to write about His transfiguration without feeling His pain.

What the three apostles saw was not Jesus' inward agonizing struggle with imminent death but His glory, as the great lawgiver and the fiercely loyal prophet commune with their Master. "Who is this rabbi of ours that even Moses and Elijah communicate so intimately with Him?" Who is He? "This is my beloved Son. Listen to Him," Yahweh's voice thunders through the silence, as if answering their unspoken question.

From one angle, the apostles needed this heavenly endorsement, testifying to the divine nature of Jesus' mission, even if they were not yet able to accept his divinity. Jesus knew only too well how weak His closest friends were. He knew they would deny and betray Him, that they would run from Him in panic. Bolstering the faith of these three key apostles was necessary because they, especially Peter, would later on be the ones to keep the others together, to be their strength, as Peter, though now so weak, would always be their immovable rock.

One would think that after witnessing this powerful testimony, especially the Father's endorsement of His Son, the apostles would be confirmed in loyalty to Jesus, but it was not very long afterward that in fear and panic they fled from His side and hid out of fear for their own lives. How frail, how weak we humans are! Jesus understood it so well, and even with pity He could say of us all, "The spirit is willing, but the flesh is weak." What a beautiful God we have, who knows us so well and still loves us, asking in return only for our friendship, as empty and inadequate as it is for Him. He is content with so little.

If You Want to Lead, Learn to Serve

An argument arose among them [the apostles] as to who was the greatest among them. Jesus knew what they were thinking. Lk 9:46–47

And when they came to Capernaum and arrived at the house, he asked them, "What were you arguing about on the road?" They said nothing because they were arguing which of them was the greatest. So he sat down and called the Twelve of them to him and said, "Whoever wants to be first must become the last and be the servant of all the rest." He then took a little child, set him in front of them, put his arms around him, and said to them, "Anyone who welcomes one of these little children in my name, welcomes me, and anyone who welcomes me welcomes not me, but the one who sent me." Mk 9:33–37

WHAT KIND OF MEN WERE THESE APOSTLES? Jesus had just recently been transfigured before their very eyes and had conversed with Moses and Elijah. Afterward He told them of His approaching arrest, torture, and death, and as if they did not hear Him they became involved in a hot dispute over who was the most important among them. Who would be in control if anything happened to their Master? I am sure they were not unconcerned about the possibility that Jesus was right in foreseeing His imminent death. Maybe it was just too heavy a burden for them to accept, much less to dwell on. Perhaps their discussion about who was most important was just idle chatter for lack of anything of importance to talk about. Whatever the motive, the thought that they might lose Jesus did cross their minds. Jesus must have been walking a bit ahead of them, as He later made believe He hadn't heard them. But He was concerned enough to bring up the issue. He was afraid that after He left them they might not treat people with the delicacy and tenderness He had always shown to everyone. Even though He was God, He had a lot of respect for people. In another version of the episode He comments that the important people of this world love to lord it over their subjects and make their importance felt. "It cannot be that way with you," He told them. "Whoever wants to be first among you must be willing to be the servant of all the rest." And He again set before them the image of a simple child, reminding them that the kingdom of heaven is for the humble, simple folk, not the self-important and the self-righteous.

And it is not just the apostles who had a problem with humility and self-promotion. We all to varying degrees tend to be that way. I have seen judges in court almost gleeful that guilty people come before them frightened and in dread of a severe disposition of their case. I have also seen instances in which a judge confronts a person who knows he is innocent and refuses to cower before the judge. It appears that the judge isn't used to feeling like he is less of a person than the defendant, and he wants to reestablish his own sense of self-importance and mastery. So the judge provokes the defendant to make an imprudent remark so that he can then cut the defendant down to size.

It is a rare person who has been promoted and given authority over others who can respond with humility and treat others with the respect that is due them based on their talents and abilities, recognizing that other people are important to making his or her own position of authority as supervisor or manager successful. Jesus Himself had authority, but we don't think of Jesus as a person who exercised authority. Yet no one ever had authority like Jesus. He exercised His authority with such delicate humility that it did not even look like authority. He never treated people as if they were beneath Him. He exercised authority by teaching beautiful, comforting messages, by healing troubled bodies and souls, by giving sight to blind people, by warning people of dangerous things that could hurt them and jeopardize their spiritual health and their future. He exercised authority by example, by the way He treated others, without ever issuing a decree or a condemnation. His greatest authority came from the transforming power of His love. It changed people's hearts and eventually their lives forever. He hoped His apostles would one day follow His example and exercise authority by the way they lived their own lives and the care they showed their flocks.

What a Strange Choice as Messenger
of the Good News

On the way to Galilee, Jesus came to the Samaritan town of Sychar, near the land that Jacob gave to his son Joseph. Jacob's well is there, and Jesus, tired from his journey, sat down by the well. It was about noon. When a Samaritan woman came out to draw water, Jesus said to her, "Would you give me a drink." His disciples had gone into the town to buy food. The Samaritan woman said to him, "You, a Jew, are asking me, a Samaritan, for a drink?" Remember, Jews do not talk to Samaritans. Jesus said, "If you only knew what God is offering you, and who it is who is asking you for a drink, you would have asked him, and he would have given you living water."

"You have no bucket, sir," she answered, "and the well is deep. How can you get this living water? Are you greater than our father Jacob, who gave us this well and drank from it himself with his sons and his animals?" Jesus replied, "Whoever drinks this water will thirst again, but whoever drinks the water I shall give will never thirst again. The water I shall give will become a wellspring within him, flowing into eternal life."

"Sir, give me that water so that I will never get thirsty and never have to come out here to draw water." "Go and call your husband and come back here," Jesus said to her. The woman said to him, "Sir, I don't have a husband." "You are right. You do not have a husband. You have had five husbands, and the one you are living with now is not your husband. You have spoken the truth." "I can see you are a prophet, sir," the woman said. "Our fathers worshipped on this mountain, while you say that Jerusalem is the place where one should worship."

Jesus said, "Woman, believe me, the time is coming when you will worship the Father neither on this mountain nor in Jerusalem. You worship what you do not know. We worship what we know. Salvation comes from the Jews. But the time will come, and indeed it is already here, when true wor-

*shippers will worship the Father in spirit and truth.
That is the kind of worship the Father wants. God
is spirit and those who worship must worship in
spirit and truth."*

*The woman said to him, "I know that the Mes-
siah is coming, and when he comes he will tell us
everything." Jesus said to her, "I, who am speaking
to you, am he."*

*At this point the disciples returned and were
surprised to see him speaking to a woman, though
none of them asked, "What do you want from her?"
or "Why are you talking to her?" The woman put
down the water jar and ran back to the village to
tell the people, "Come out and meet a man who
told me about everything I ever did. I wonder, could
he be the Messiah?" The people left the village and
went out to see him.* JN 4:5–30

THERE IS SO MUCH PACKED INTO THIS VERY STAR-
tling event. First of all it again reveals Jesus' uncanny
knowledge of details in people's lives, even of events that
have not yet taken place. He knew that the woman would
be at that well. His arrival there was perfectly timed. As
He approached the well He sent the apostles on their way

to buy provisions. A short time later the woman arrived at the well to draw water. Usually women gathered at the well in early morning while it was still cool. This woman was clearly an outcast and was made to feel unwelcome by the nice people in town, so she would go out to the well when there would be no one there, at high noon, when the sun was the hottest. Jesus knew all about her. He knew her pain. And He knew she would be there, and He was waiting for her. He asked her for a drink of water. And a sharp conversation ensued. Jesus asked to meet her husband. "I do not have a husband," she said. "You are right; you do not have a husband," Jesus said. "You have had five husbands and the man you are living with now is not your husband." He did not say it critically, nor did the woman take it as a critical remark.

When Jesus had been confronted by the Pharisees on the matter of divorce previously, He proclaimed in no uncertain terms that marriage was indissoluble, and that divorce had been forbidden by God from the beginning. He preached a very high ideal of the marriage bond. Here he met this woman, a Samaritan no less, who didn't have a spotless reputation among her neighbors. Interesting! He said, "You have had five husbands," recognizing, though not approving, that she had been married five times, and that the man she was presently living with she had never bothered to marry. The woman was impressed, and brought up the subject of the Messiah who would reveal many things. Then Jesus came up with the stunning admission that He was the Messiah. That is the only time He ever revealed so directly that He was the Messiah. Peter received his understanding of Jesus' identity from God, not from Jesus. Jesus did say to the people in Nazareth that Isaiah's prophecy about the Messiah was being fulfilled as He spoke. But in this instance He told the woman who He was in perfectly clear terms. Look at what she was! Why tell her? Why not tell one of the nice people in town? Because He could see beneath the surface of her life, that she *was* a nice person, that there was much goodness in her that others could not see, as He judges by what He sees in people's hearts. And the woman did just what Jesus knew she would do, and what He intended she should do. She left her bucket on the well and ran to tell the villagers the whole story. "Come out and meet a man who told me about my whole past life. Could He be the Messiah?" Jesus chose that woman to be the messenger of the Good News to that village. He handpicked her to be a missionary, an apostle to the Samaritans. And look at what she was! Can you imagine picking a person like that to be a reader in church, or even to be on the parish council, or to speak in church? What would Jesus do? What did Jesus do?

This story reveals so much about Jesus. He could

preach the highest of ideals, as on marriage, and then come across a person who fell far short of the ideal and show exquisite compassion and understanding. He did not see this woman as evil, but as possessed of much goodness, and He chose her to be the missionary to that village. So often we self-righteously insist on people observing the high ideals we preach, but we are without mercy when people fall short of those ideals, and we think they should be cut off from God. We see clearly in this story that we have fallen far short of Jesus' ideal for us: to show mercy and compassion for those who fall short in our estimation. We tend to judge only by what we see on the surface; we fail to look into people's hearts to see the goodness that lies there. We have much to learn from the Good Shepherd, about how He differs from the scribes and Pharisees. And another interesting detail. The Gospel says nothing about Jesus telling the woman to give up the person she was living with. If He had demanded that, what would have happened to the woman? After six men, how old was she? Who would have wanted her? What would have been left for her? Perhaps just to wander homeless. Here we have another example of the Good Shepherd's exquisite compassion for those who fall far short of our ideals.

Don't Be Discouraged If
Success Comes Slowly

"Now listen, the sower went out to sow. As he sowed, some seeds fell by the wayside, and the birds came and ate them up. Other seeds fell upon rocky ground, where there was not much soil. They sprang up right away, but because the soil had no depth when the sun rose they were scorched, and with no chance for roots to grow they withered. Other seeds fell among thornbushes. When the thornbushes spread, they choked the seeds. Other seeds fell upon fertile soil and yielded fruit, some a hundredfold, some sixtyfold, some thirtyfold. Listen to what I am telling you." MT 13:4–9

JESUS WEAVES SO MUCH PSYCHOLOGY INTO HIS PARA-
bles. He is talking about His message of Good News.
He is not optimistic about the prospects for an abundant
harvest, nor is He pessimistic. He is a hard realist. He
knows precisely what is going to happen as a result of all
His hard work. His message will not even have a chance
with most people, for various reasons. When they first hear
Him some are impressed. It is Good News, it is new. They
embrace it for a while, but there are so many other interests. Others are attracted to this Good News. They commit themselves to it, but it creates too many problems for
them, and they drift away. Still others like the Good News,
but life is so difficult and there are so many other problems to contend with. A percentage, however, will accept
His message, embrace it, and it will take hold and produce
abundant fruit, in various quantities.

His understanding of the human heart held no illu-
sions. He knew most people who showed a lot of enthusi-
asm in the beginning were coming to Him not to believe in
Him but because they were curious, or because He had
the power to heal every kind of disease and illness. He
knew few of these people would ever be ready to make a
lifelong commitment to His teaching. He knew what was
in the human heart. He fashioned it. So He had no illu-
sions as to what He could expect.

In this parable He is telling us about the successes and

failures of His own efforts to bring His Good News to His people, but He is also offering important insights into our own endeavors here on earth.

Each of us struggles to make our dreams a reality. We have to dream. Dreams are the breath of the soul. Fulfilling dreams is not always our responsibility, nor is it always within our power. There we need a partner, and that is the beautiful thing about God. Most people never realize it, but God wants to be our partner. He is the one who made us; He gave us a mission to accomplish and seeds to plant. We do the dreaming. He takes our dreams and works quietly and intimately with us to make our dreams become reality. To keep a good partnership going with Him, we need to be humble and patient in sharing our dreams with Him and allowing Him to work in us and with us. But we have to leave the results entirely in His hands. Only He can give life to our dreams. Without Him we just stumble along with our little dreams but they never burst into full-blown masterpieces of creation until we allow God to give them life. He doesn't intrude. We have to want Him in our life. For Jesus, His Father was always His Partner, and even then only in time did His dreams blossom, as not everyone was ready to receive what He had to give.

It is the same with us. Each of us has something important to contribute to the world. We struggle as we give birth to whatever it is that God wants to give to the world through our efforts. Often we can feel like Jesus. He tried to spread His message, but so few were interested. We can feel His frustration as we try to share with others what God has shared with us. We realize after much effort that that is done best with God as an intimate part of our life. It is then that life becomes an adventure and not an exercise that seems futile. But, then, God does not view success the way we view success. We measure success by the results. God is the one who gives the success. Often His plans for us might be just to plant the seed for someone else to reap the harvest. For that reason it is healthy for us to have a certain detachment from the work we know God wants us to do. Just doing the work may be all He has planned for us. He may entrust the fulfillment to others who may understand what we have begun and are better positioned to bring it to fruition.

The Prodigal Father

Jesus said, "There was a man who had two sons. The younger of them said to his father, 'Give me my share of the inheritance that will be coming to me.' And he divided his living between them.

"Not long after the younger son gathered all he had and took off for a country far away. There he squandered his property in loose living. When he had spent everything, a great famine arose in that country, and he began to feel want. So he went and joined himself to one of the citizens of that country, who sent him into his field to feed swine. He would gladly have fed on the pods that the swine ate, but no one gave him anything. When he finally came to himself, he said, 'How many of my father's servants have bread enough and to spare while I perish here with hunger. I will rise and go to my father, and say to him, "Father, I have sinned against heaven and before you. I am no longer worthy to be called your son. Treat me as one of your hired servants." '

"And he arose and went to his father. But while he was still at a distance his father saw him and had compassion, and ran and embraced him and kissed him. And the son said to him, 'Father, I have sinned against heaven and before you. I am no longer worthy to be called your son.' But the father said to his servants, 'Bring quickly the best robe, and put it on him, and put a ring on his hand, and shoes on his feet, and bring the fatted calf and kill it, and let us eat and make merry, for my son who was dead is now alive again. He was lost and has been found.' And they began to celebrate.

"Now the older son was in the field, and as he was coming home and approaching the house he heard the music and saw the dancing. Calling one of the servants, he asked him what it meant. And he said to him, 'Your brother has come home and your father has killed the fatted calf because he returned safely.' But he was angry and refused to go in. His father came out and begged him, but he told his father, 'All these many years have I served you and

> *never disobeyed your orders, yet you never gave me
> so much as a kid goat to party with my friends. But
> now that this son of yours has come who has wasted
> your living with harlots, you kill the fatted calf for
> him.' And the father said to him, 'Son, you are with
> me always, and all that I have is yours. It was only
> right that we should rejoice and celebrate, for your
> brother was dead and is now alive. He was lost and
> is found.'"* LK 15:11–32

T HIS PARABLE HAS ALWAYS BEEN KNOWN AS THE
parable of the prodigal son. I think it has been misunderstood. Jesus intended the key person in the parable to
be not the son but the father. It is the father who is prodigal. What father would give in to a son who demanded his
inheritance long before his father died? What a brash,
nervy fellow! And the father goes along with him and divides his property. What kind of a father is that? Either he
loves his kids to an extreme or he is just a foolish man.
Now think of how lavishly God pours out His gifts and talents and riches into our lives. What do we do with all that
inheritance He has given us, which we have done nothing
to earn? Do we use all that treasure for Him and for the
benefit of others? How much of our lives have we wasted?

After he had squandered his fortune, destitute, starving, and lost, the young man set out on his journey back home to his father. Was he really repentant? Possibly, but his carefully crafted speech to his father makes him look more like a shrewd character than a heartbroken penitent. And as he approached the vast estate, the father, who seemingly had gone out every day to look over the horizon hoping to spot his son in the distance, on this occasion saw a tiny figure on the horizon. He just knew it was his son. It was his son finally come home. And what did he do? He ran out with a few of his servants and before the kid even had a chance to say a word, he hugged him, kissed him, and, smelling the stench of his unwashed son, told the servants to bring him inside, wash him down, put a new robe on him, a ring on his finger, sandals on his feet, and kill the fatted calf and prepare a grand celebration because his son who was lost and presumed dead had come home alive and well.

What father in his right mind would do that? I don't know of any. Maybe a mother would. Any father would at least say to the kid, "Well, kid, did you finally learn your lesson?" and then he would wait for the son to give an apology or some expression of sorrow for his selfish, sinful ways. But not this father. He was being unreasonable in lavishing love on this spoiled rotten kid.

You cannot help but get the feeling that Jesus is telling

us about His Father and the kind of unconditional love He has for us, His human children, on whom He lavishes all His riches and from whom He asks very little in return— just as the father in the parable treated his son. It is a kind of love that most humans, especially men, would scoff at as ridiculous. And we, like the son, waste all that God gives us on ourselves and what we can get out of life. Like the son, when we have finished seeking our own will in all things and are hurting, we come back to Him with what few crumbs we have left. And the Father asks us for nothing; He is just happy we have come home. What a God! What a helpless, hopeless God whose love no weak, petty human mind could ever comprehend!

Jesus is trying to convince His disciples not to be afraid of His Father, and their Father in heaven. He is nothing like the angry, punishing God they might have learned about as children. His love is so far beyond what we could even begin to imagine.

Yes, we are all prodigal children. And there will always be the self-righteous people who supposedly have never done anything wrong and who resent the return to grace of the wretched penitent who is restored to the Father's love and is, in their eyes, unjustly rewarded.

I Need to Be Alone

The Jewish Feast of Tabernacles was approaching, and Jesus' brethren said to him, "Leave here and go to Judea so your disciples may see the works you are doing. For no one who wants to become famous works in secret. If you do these things, you show yourself to the world." Even his brethren did not believe in him. Jesus said to them, "My time has not yet come, but your time is always here. The world cannot hate you, but it hates me because I testify against it that its works are evil. Go to the feast yourselves. I am not going up to the feast, for it is not yet my time."

After his brethren had gone up to the feast, he then left on his own, not publicly, but in private. The Judeans were looking for him at the feast, and

> *saying, "Where is he?" And there was much gossip*
> *about him among the people. Some were saying,*
> *"He is a good man," while others were saying, "No,*
> *he is leading the people astray." Yet, for fear of the*
> *Judean officials, no one spoke openly of him.*
> JN 7:2–13

W HAT A RARE GLIMPSE INTO AN INTIMATE FAMILY
scene involving Jesus! He is home in Galilee with
His family. They are discussing details of their planned trip
to Jerusalem for the Feast of Tents, or Tabernacles. Jesus
does not seem interested. "What's the matter? Is there
something wrong? Is something troubling you? If you want
to become well-known, this is the time and the place to
declare yourself. The whole world will be there. Are you all
right?" "You go and enjoy yourselves," Jesus tells them. "I'm
not going. It is not my time yet."

It is a strange scene. Once His family members have
departed He started off on His own. That also is very hard
to understand. What is the reason? Why would He not
want to go with His family and relatives in the caravan for
this joyful feast in Jerusalem? Did He need to be alone
with His thoughts? Was He depressed? Did He just not
want to go along with the caravan from Galilee with every-

one asking questions? Did He foresee something that He did not want to talk about? Did He imagine that a large caravan of Galileans entering Jerusalem with Him prominently in their midst could start trouble? Jesus knew that the people, especially the mobs, were looking for excitement, and He did not want to be forced into being part of a public spectacle that wouldn't further His work and could be dangerous.

Going alone unannounced was better. That way He could mingle with the people quietly and enjoy the feast. It was the yearly harvest celebration, and hordes of pilgrims from far and wide, many from other countries, would be gathering around Jerusalem, living in tents all along the hillside and across the valley. It was a happy time when Galileans and Israelites would renew old friendships and make new friends. He had always since childhood cherished happy memories of this feast. If He came alone there might still be some who did not know Him personally, so He could relax and enjoy socializing with them, especially those from distant lands.

This feast was a reminder of the years His ancestors spent wandering in the desert on their long journey to the Promised Land. It was not as solemn as Passover, and people were more inclined to become involved in discussing the latest goings-on throughout the country and in Jerusalem itself. What was the latest news? What has become of that new itinerant rabbi, Jesus, we've been hearing about? Are the officials going to embrace Him? Or do they consider Him dangerous? Do you think He will be coming to the feast? The whole populace would be talking about Him and hoping to get at least a glimpse of this famous teacher. He foresaw all this chatter and thrilled at the chance to walk anonymously among them. It would be only too soon before someone would recognize Him and then the temporary peace would end and the turmoil would flare up all over again. These must have been the thoughts crossing Jesus' mind as the family, the apostles included, set out on the long journey. He was glad to be going alone. He needed the peace and quiet, even though it would be short-lived. There would not be many more such opportunities in the short time He had left.

It seems that Jesus was able to maintain His anonymity for at least a few days. Then, in the middle of the feast when His presence had become known, He went up into the Temple to teach, and the professional Temple scholars who may have heard about Him but had never met him were so impressed with His teaching that they remarked to each other, "How is it that this man has learning when He has never studied?" They would have known that He had not studied because they were the scholars and anyone interested in scholarly learning would have had to pass through their courses on Scripture and the Law. They were the ones who certified the teachers. This unknown scholar they had never seen in their classes. Where did He get all this wisdom and learning? Apparently these men were out of touch with the more political priests and Pharisees. They seemed to be unfamiliar with Jesus and the fury stirring around Him, and they did not readily recognize who He was.

As Jesus was speaking to the crowd that had gathered around Him, already other scribes and Pharisees and priests who knew Him were circulating among the crowd. Jesus spotted them and immediately began to address them, while still responding to the scholars who had been listening. "You do not know me, because my learning is not my own, but is from He who sent me. Anyone who does His will will know whether my teaching is from God or whether I am teaching on my own authority." And then, turning His glance toward the political leaders, He continued, "Moses gave you the Law, and yet you do not keep the Law. And furthermore why do you want to kill me?" This infuriated the Pharisees and shortly afterward, when their couriers got their messages back to the chief priests, soldiers came out to arrest Jesus. However, for some reason they did not carry out their orders, because they went back to the chief priests empty-handed.

This was just what Jesus was hoping would not happen. He enjoyed talking with the real Temple scholars.

They seemed very open to what He had to say and apparently had no trouble accepting His teachings. They were impressed, and then the political element showed up and the peaceful interlude ended. This must have been so frustrating for Jesus. All He wanted to do was give a beautiful message of Good News from God to His people, yet wherever He went there was trouble. Jesus knew it was the work of Satan, working through his stooges, the religious leaders, who hounded Him at every step. The harassment would have driven a lesser man to madness. But Jesus always kept a cool, detached attitude, knowing full well that the drama that was taking place beneath the surface was the prelude to the final struggle between good and evil, between God and the powers of hell. And He also knew what the outcome would be. So He maintained His calm, cool demeanor. But beneath it all there seems to be sadness in Him, a sadness that came from wanting to give so much to the people, but the people were not in the right frame of mind and didn't have the readiness of heart to accept what He was offering.

Violence Does Not Resolve Issues;
It Breeds Nightmares

*"Put back the sword into its sheath. Those who live
by the sword will perish by the sword."* MT 26:52

I NEVER PAID MUCH ATTENTION TO THIS PASSAGE UN-
til recently, nor did I notice the powerful messages
behind Jesus' words. Jesus spoke these words when a detachment of Temple guards came to arrest Him. It was
seemingly Peter who drew his sword to defend Jesus, cut-
ting off the ear of the high priest's servant. Jesus healed
the man wounded by the sword and sent a warning to
those who resort to violence as a means of settling a dispute. The sword was, until not very long ago, a common

weapon of war. Jesus' warning on this occasion applies to all times, whatever weapon is used. Violence is not the way to settle disputes. Animals settle disputes by physical violence because they have nothing like our human intelligence. Violence is most often their way of meeting a threat. Humans have intelligence, and our means of resolving issues are limited only by our imaginations and our determination to resolve our problems intelligently without resorting to brute force. No matter how technologically advanced and exciting and glamorous our weaponry may be, it is still brute force and still a crude and barbaric way to resolve problems. Even when conflicts do escalate into violence, bloodshed does not resolve the original issue but merely creates new and often much more threatening problems, to say nothing of the damage that is done to God's children, and that damage is always catastrophic. Besides the dead, there is always the horrible physical, psychological, and moral damage to the wounded and their families, with the pain often lasting for the rest of their lives. And the most horrible premise behind war is that humans are dispensable. At the end of the conflict the costs are shown in stark figures. Whatever was gained cannot outweigh the incalculable and far-reaching damage done to human beings. The hatred generated by war spreads like a pandemic to other peoples not even directly involved in the conflict, and plants the seeds for future conflicts. So the wisdom Jesus expressed in such a brief sentence is vast in its vision of the far-reaching consequences of violent conflict. The possibility that our planet could be destroyed by humans resorting to violence to resolve disputes is far more likely than the rare chance that it could be destroyed by some natural cataclysm. "Those who live by the sword will perish by the sword." They are not just words, but the vision of God and His warning to all of us.

And even when a violent response is justifiable against a violent and evil aggressor, the overall damage is still devastating, and the price is still high. It would be for the betterment of the whole of civilization for us never to end the search for alternatives to violence.

Do What the Scribes and Pharisees Tell You, but Do Not Imitate Them!

As it happened, Jesus was passing between Samaria and Galilee on his way to Jerusalem. As he was entering a certain village he was met by ten lepers who were standing at a distance. They called out to him, crying, "Jesus, Master, have pity on us." When he saw them he said, "Go, show yourselves to the priests." As they were on their way, they were made clean. One of them, seeing that he was made clean, returned, glorifying God with a loud voice. He fell on his face at Jesus' feet, giving thanks, and he was a Samaritan.

Jesus answered and said, "Were not the ten made clean? Where are the nine? Has no one been found to return and give glory to God except this foreigner?" And he said to him, "Arise, go on your way. Your faith has saved you." Lk 17:11–19

INTERESTING! ISRAELITES AND SAMARITANS WERE forbidden to associate with each other. There was a wall of hatred between them. Yet leprosy broke down that wall. There were no social barriers separating lepers from fellow lepers. They were just forbidden to associate with nice people. They saw friends to be loved in each other, and they gathered in groups for support and companionship, in this case Galileans and Samaritans, and who knows what other kinds of nondescripts.

They heard Jesus was coming. His reputation had spread all throughout the Roman province of Syria, so there was hardly a soul who had not heard of this famous preacher who could heal the most hideous diseases, even flesh-eating leprosy. So, keeping their distance, the lepers yelled out to him, "Jesus, heal us." And responding to their soulful plea, He told them to go and show themselves to the priests, so they could be declared clean.

This is another important gesture on Jesus' part. The priests treated Jesus in a rude and vicious manner, yet Jesus did not respond in kind. They were the teaching authority appointed by His Father, so He had to set an example by respecting them. He told the lepers to do what the priests ordered—to show themselves to the priests when they had been healed of the disease. I am sure it was not an easy thing for Jesus to show respect for a corrupt priesthood, but He always did.

When they have a problem with priests or with the way they run the Church, so many people just leave the Church, and in doing that they walk away from the precious kingdom of God that Jesus gave us, and for which He told us we should be willing to sacrifice everything. As crudely as the Jewish priests treated Him, Jesus was still loyal to the religion His Father had established, and He insisted His followers be loyal to it. He attended the synagogue services and kept the feasts and respected the religious leaders, even though He knew they were trying to destroy Him.

His Ways Are Not Our Ways

"The kingdom of heaven is like a vine grower who went out early in the morning to hire laborers for his vineyard. He agreed with the laborers for a denarius a day, and sent them into his vineyard. At about nine o'clock he went out and saw others standing idle in the marketplace, so he said to them, 'Go into my vineyard and I will pay you what is just.' So they went. Again he went out at about noon and at three o'clock and did the same. At about five o'clock he went out again and still found others standing around, so he said to them, 'Why are you all standing here all day idle?' They said to him, 'Because no one has hired us.' So he said to them, 'You also go into my vineyard.'

"When evening came, the owner said to the

steward, 'Call the workers and pay them their
wages, beginning from the last even to the first.'
When those who started at five o'clock came they
each received a denarius. When those who started
work first came, they thought they would receive
more, but they received each a denarius. On receiv-
ing it they were disappointed and began to com-
plain against the owner, saying, 'These worked but
a single hour and you put them on a level with us,
who have borne the burden of the day's heat.' But in
answer to them he said, 'Friend, I did you no injustice. Did you not agree with me for a denarius?
Take what is yours and go. I choose to give to these
last the same as you. Do I not have a right to do as I
choose, or are you envious because I am so generous? I tell you, the first will be last and the last first,
for many are called but few are chosen.' "

Mt 20:1–16

T HIS PARABLE REMINDS ME OF THE PARABLE ABOUT
the prodigal son, or as I like to call it, the parable of
the prodigal father. That parable and this one are internally
connected. Jesus is drawing us into God's mind. It is only
after many years of pondering Jesus' words that we can begin to put His thoughts together in a way that can make

sense to our feeble human minds and shabby human values. Listening to Jesus is like being drawn deeper and deeper into the ocean of God's mind. It's a world that is so foreign to our ordinary human way of thinking and our ordering of human values. In the parable about the prodigal father and in this parable about the vine grower, there are the dedicated hardworking laborers and the Johnny-come-latelies. The latecomers seem to have it made. They are the ones who seem to reap the reward. The prodigal son is given a big party and accepted back into the family. His hardworking brother, so dedicated to his father, seems to have been overlooked. In the parable about the vine grower the workers who came later were given the same pay as the ones who had worked since daybreak and during the worst heat of the day. In comparing this scenario to the Kingdom of God, Jesus challenges our human way of thinking. This setup doesn't make sense to us. We know that God is not unjust. We know that He is not ungrateful toward those who are loyal to Him and struggle hard to be good. We know that there is no way that shrewd people are going to make a fool out of God. So what is Jesus trying to tell us? What is He revealing to us about God's mind and God's values?

To bring this into our modern world, recall many years ago a member of a criminal organization was sent to Sing Sing prison for murder. While he was on death row awaiting his execution, the prison chaplain visited him often.

Eventually, the prisoner, who was Jewish, asked the priest if he could be baptized and become a Catholic. The priest instructed him in what it meant to be Christian, to accept Jesus as his Savior and be genuinely sorry for all the evil he had done, and to be willing to forgive all his enemies. When the priest was convinced the conversion was genuine, he baptized the prisoner and gave him Holy Communion. A short time later the man was executed in the electric chair.

Many good Christians were irate that the priest had baptized the criminal and made his entrance into heaven so easy. They knew that sincere conversion and baptism washes away all sins and punishment for sin, and if death follows shortly after, the person goes immediately to heaven.

Why were such seemingly good people offended? Why was the brother of the prodigal son offended? Why were the laborers who endured the long hours of work in the vineyard offended? Because they struggled hard to be faithful and to do a good job, and those who were less deserving were richly rewarded. They felt unappreciated, as if the father in one case, the owner of the vineyard in the other case, and God Himself in the third case were ungrateful and uncaring about their hard work.

Why does Jesus lead us down that path when the lesson is so difficult for us to understand? What is He trying to tell us? That God is unjust, ungrateful, or unappreciative of good people's loyalty and hard work? That doesn't make sense. I suppose the answer lies in what God knows about the rewards He has prepared for all of us. Only He knows what is in store for us in heaven. The first thing we have to learn is the immensity of God's compassion for all of us. None of us is that glowingly loyal or dedicated to God and generous in giving to God what He would really like from all of us. Nor are any of us that heroically holy that we can set ourselves far above any other sinner as deserving of a much greater reward from God than a sinner who is more notorious in God's eyes. What is really important to God is that a soul He loves, a soul that could be lost for eternity, finally responds to His grace and comes back home to His love. Unfortunately, we are not enough in love with God to share in His joy over the return of a lost soul. The angels rejoice over the return of a sinner, Jesus tells us. The whole family of God should rejoice. Our inability to rejoice is a reflection on us and not an indictment of God's sense of fairness. And when we finally experience the reward that awaits us in heaven, we will then know that we have not been cheated. Those who considered themselves more deserving than others, such as the scribes and Pharisees, will find themselves not so deserving at the end and will be surprised to find themselves in lower places than those they considered undeserving. Many are called but few are chosen—not through God's fault, but through our own.

No Rest for the Weary

Jesus and his disciples withdrew to the sea. A great crowd followed him. They were people from Gali-lee, and Judea, and from Jerusalem, and Idumea, and from beyond the Jordan. A large crowd from the vicinity of Tyre and Sidon, hearing about what he was doing, came to him. He told his disciples to have a small boat ready for him because of the crowd, which was almost trampling him, for he was healing so many that as many as had ailments were pressing upon him to touch him. And the unclean spirits who drove their victims to impurity, when-ever they beheld him, they fell down before him and cried out, "You are the Son of God." He ordered them not to make him known. MK 3:7–12

E VEN THOUGH THIS SNAPSHOT IS SO SMALL, IT RE-
veals a lot. Galilee, Judea, Idumea, the land beyond
the Jordan (Perea), even Tyre and Sidon—look at a map of
Palestine and see the vast area these regions comprise, and
you get a glimpse of how far and wide Jesus' reputation
had spread. Starting up north in pagan country, the land of
the Philistines, present-day Lebanon, people had heard of
him way up there. Then going down and mentioning
Galilee, and though it is not mentioned there must also
have been Samaritans as Jesus was very popular in Samaria. There were also followers from Judea and Idumea
and the land across the Jordan. Large crowds from all
those lands followed Jesus around like sheep. That is why
the image of sheep and shepherd kept popping up in His
mind and in His conversation. The people were like a flock
of wandering sheep, not knowing where to go. Why did
they come flocking to Him? Basically for one reason: because He had a reputation for healing illnesses of all sorts,
including fatal illnesses, curing even lepers and people
born blind, people for whom doctors were hopeless. Even
pagans who did not believe in God reached out to Him.
They cared little where His power came from. All they
knew was that He could heal, and it was real. Many even
among the pagans found faith eventually. Later on we see
flourishing communities of Christians in the previously pagan countries nearby. And the Idumeans, the Bedouins
who thrived on selling cheeses, goats' milk, wool, rugs, and

other animal products—even they followed Jesus around. And it was not just the healings that drew them. If that was the only reason, they would have come and gone after they got what they wanted. But they continued to follow Him for what He had to give them, what they and all humans crave: a reason to live, peace of mind and soul, a realization that they are precious to God—not the frightening deity they thought they knew, but the tender Father Jesus revealed to them. They loved to hear from His lips that they were the children of a Father who loved them, and for whom He had sent His Son to ransom them from the Evil One and reconcile them to Himself in heaven. Each person knew by the look in Jesus' eyes that He knew and loved him or her as a dear friend. They felt proud, and that knowledge gave them peace, so they clung to Him like little children. They did not want to let Him leave. They followed Him everywhere. What a motley crew! Never before had they gotten along on their own with one another, but in Jesus' friendship they were no longer hostile strangers; they were slowly perhaps but surely becoming friends, and forming Jesus' first family. Even those people from across the Jordan, the land of Sodom and Gomorrah, with their own unique culture and customs and strange architecture, became part of this nondescript family, the seeds of the Kingdom of God on earth.

It is amazing how barriers break down when Jesus is presented to people, even people who are not Christian. When *Joshua,* a book I wrote, first came out, Hindu monks from India sent for cases of *Joshua* books for their libraries. Jesus' message had deeply touched their lives. So many letters came to me from Jewish people telling me they fell in love with Jesus through reading *Joshua.* Many of them asked if they could learn more and whether I could baptize them secretly.

One day a group of Hindus from near where I live asked could they meet with me and would I talk to them about Jesus. They were professional people—engineers, doctors, psychiatrists, and others. They had read *Joshua* and realized it was about Jesus, and they wanted to know more. I talked to them for about two hours. I think there were over thirty people at that meeting. When I finished speaking they asked me where they should go from there. They wanted more. They were thirsting for what Jesus had to give them. The whole world seems to crave what Jesus has to give, and when Jesus is presented to them people can't get enough. They don't want to learn about the teachings of a church or an institution. They want to meet the real Jesus and learn what He is really like. They want to be part of Him and follow Him like all the people in that Gospel passage. If we try to substitute the doctrines of an institution we are then teaching them the medium of the message and not the message. Jesus is the message. The institution, the Church, is the medium of the message. We have to make it possible for people to meet the real Jesus, the Jesus about whom the apostles taught when they brought the first pagans to Christianity. Jesus will always satisfy the deepest needs of the human heart, because He alone knows what the heart and soul need. He made us. All the things He taught can be absorbed later, once people have grown to know Him better.

Storm Clouds over the Last Supper

It was before the feast of Passover. Jesus knew that the hour had come for him to pass from this world and go to the Father. He had always loved those who were his in the world, but now he showed how perfect his love was.

They were at supper and the devil had already deceived Judas into betraying him. Jesus knew that the Father had put everything in his hands, and that he had come from God and was returning to God. He got up from the table, removed his tunic, and dressed like a slave, wrapping a towel around his waist. He then poured water into a basin and began to wash the feet of the disciples and wipe them with the towel he was wearing.

As he came to Simon Peter, Peter said to him,

*"Lord, are you going to wash my feet?" Jesus an-
swered, "Now you do not understand what I am doing, but one day you will." "Never," Peter said. "You
will never wash my feet." Jesus replied, "If I do not
wash your feet, you can have no part with me."
"Then, Lord, wash not only my feet, but my face
and hands too." Jesus said, "No one who has bathed
has need to wash, he is already clean. You too are
clean, though not all of you are." He knew who was
to betray him. That was why he had said "though
not all of you are."*

*When he had washed their feet and put on his
clothes again, he went back to the table and said to
them, "Do you understand what I have just done to
you? You call me Master and Lord, and rightly so,
for so I am. But if I, the Lord and Master, can wash
your feet, you should wash the feet of one another. I
have given you an example of how you should imitate what I have done for you."* JN 13:1–15

E VEN AS HE WAS ABOUT TO LEAVE THIS WORLD
Jesus was still concerned about the apostles' ability to
treat His disciples with humility and to rule them gently.
This act of self-abasement on Jesus' part at the Last Supper could break the hardest of hearts. This is God, the

Creator of the universe, stripping to the clothes of a slave and getting on his knees with a towel and basin of water and humbly washing the feet of His own creatures, because He was afraid they would not be able to even begin to approach the humility He had shown toward the simple unwashed masses whom He had so gently comforted and healed each day. He was worried about the pain of all those simple creatures whom his apostles would have to shepherd after He left to go back to His Father.

The apostles were so shocked and ashamed, they were reduced to an embarrassed silence and were totally uncomfortable witnessing a scene they would never forget, a scene Jesus wanted them never to forget. They knew why He was humbling Himself so unashamedly, because they were so proud and felt so self-important. One wonders if they weren't all in tears seeing their Master debasing Himself, imitating a slave washing his master's feet. It was too much for Peter. When Jesus reached him, he had already drawn his feet up under his robe so Jesus could not find them. Finally he acquiesced after Jesus told him that if He did not wash his feet, he could have no part with Him.

But the message of Jesus' example is not just for the apostles. It is for all of us as well. Would to God we priests would look upon God's sheep with the humility and respect and solicitude Jesus had for His troubled, suffering sheep. He knew their pain and knew only too well that so many of them had been abused and damaged from childhood. He never would have demanded of them what we demand of our people for our respect as sheep in good standing, worthy of Communion.

We have so much to learn about Jesus, but there is nowhere to learn about Him because seminaries, Catholic or Protestant, do not teach courses about Jesus, other than brief Christology courses relating the history of the development of the dogma about Jesus' identity. Why is there such resistance to learning about Jesus and how He was so different from the scribes and Pharisees? What is needed are in-depth studies about the inner life of Jesus, providing prayerful, psychological analyses of the mind and heart of Jesus as He met with all varieties of people in the Gospel stories. There are such rich, untapped treasures lying between the lines of the Gospel stories. Someday someone in authority may finally consider it worthwhile for seminarians to get to know Jesus, so that when they become priests and clergy they can have the mind and heart of the Good Shepherd. This desire weighed heavily on Jesus' heart on the night before He died. He was very much afraid that His shepherds would follow the role model of the legalistic scribes and Pharisees and run roughshod over the already badly damaged sheep; He was afraid that His priests would demand more of their people than their broken condition could bear, and in the process drive them away without hope to wander aimlessly into dangerous places.

Keep Forgiving in Spite of Yourself

Peter came up to Jesus and said, "Lord, how often shall my brother sin against me and I forgive him? Seven times?" Jesus said to him, "I do not say seven times, but seventy times seven times.

"That is why the kingdom of heaven is like to a king who decided to settle accounts with his servants. When he had begun the settlement, one was brought to him who owed him $20,000,000, and as he had no means of paying, the king ordered him to be sold with his wife and children and all that he had, as payment of the debt. But the servant fell down at his feet and begged him, 'Be patient with me and I will pay you all.' Moved with compassion, the king released him and forgave him the debt.

"But as that servant went out, he met one of his

fellow servants who owed him $200. He grabbed him and shook him, demanding, 'Pay me what you owe me!' His fellow servant fell on his knees and begged him, 'Be patient with me and I will repay you all.' But he would not, and went away and had the man put into prison until he could pay him what was his due.

"His fellow servants saw what had happened, were deeply upset, and went and informed the king of all that had occurred. Then the king summoned him and said to him, 'Wicked servant! I forgave you all the debt because you entreated me. Should you not have had pity on your fellow servant, just as I had pity on you?' And the king, being angry, handed him over to the torturers until he should pay all that he owed. So also shall my heavenly Father treat you, if you do not each forgive your fellow human beings from your heart." Mt 18:21–35

Forgiveness is at the core of Jesus' teachings. The human family collectively owes God a debt we can never possibly pay. Not only that, but each of us individually owes God a debt we can never pay. Forgiveness of debts is the reason Jesus came to earth. The debt we owe to our Creator was incurred by an offense and affront Adam and Eve committed against His majesty. There can be no adequate human compensation for this debt. Only God can satisfy what is owed, and Jesus is footing our bill. By becoming one of us, He could stand in our place, as He did when He entered the Jordan River and asked John to baptize Him. At that moment He took upon Himself the sins of us all, and became the Lamb of God who had come to offer Himself in sacrifice to atone for the sins of humanity from Adam to the last person at the end of the world.

He came to heal the rift caused by Adam's sin and to reunite us all to His Father. No easy task. His whole life was spent healing, from morning till night; that was all He did, heal people's physical ills and spiritual ills. He wanted healing to be the signature of His mission, and He sent the apostles out to heal body and spirit. He made Himself most vulnerable yet never took offense at anything anyone ever did to Him, and that was the secret to how He could always forgive, even the most horrendous of insults. That was why He told Peter that one must forgive always, not just seven times, although Peter thought that was more than enough. We are meant to forgive always, as often as a person offends us.

On the surface it seems like an impossibility, but forgiveness was Jesus' key to true inner peace, and peace throughout the world. How many crimes, how much misery, how many wars have been caused by people refusing to forgive personal injuries? Bad judgments made out of hatred and unforgiven injuries have bred wars and terrorism and evil of all sorts, and all of it hides behind the mask of justice and concern for others.

Jesus' parable about forgiveness is graphic. The king in the parable is God. Our offenses against Him are beyond recompense. There is no way we can atone. Offenses committed against His divine majesty can never be offered adequate satisfaction by our puny created status. We are fortunate that Jesus was willing to atone for us. All God expects of us are mere tokens of sorrow for the evil we do. But He does expect us to forgive our neighbors' offenses against us—and these offenses are insignificant compared to the ones we commit against Him. So when we refuse to forgive others it is a slap in God's face, because He has been so forgiving of us. To be faithful to the Creator, our judicial systems should be aimed at healing and rehabilitating those of God's children who have done evil, not destroying them. Those officials who mete out justice should be mindful of the wrath of God because one day they will come before His judgment seat. Our heavenly Father will treat them the way they have treated others.

It Is Not How Much You Make That Counts, but How Much You Give Away

A certain man came to Jesus and said, "Good Master, what good deed must I do to earn eternal life?" Jesus said to him, "Why do you call me good and ask me about what is good? God alone is good. But if you wish to enter into life, keep the commandments." "Which ones?" the man asked. And Jesus said, "You shall not kill, you shall not commit adultery, you shall not steal, you shall not bear false witness. Honor your father and mother, and you shall love your neighbor as yourself."

The young man said to Jesus, "All these things I have kept from my youth; what is still expected of me?" Jesus said to him, "If you want to be perfect, go, sell what you have and give to the poor, and you shall

have treasure in heaven, and come follow me."
When the man heard this he became sad and walked
away, for he had great possessions. Mt 19:16–22

THIS IS A VERY INTERESTING STORY BECAUSE OF Jesus' surprising response to the man's question as to what he must do to have eternal life. Keep the commandments, Jesus told him, but the last statement Jesus made was not one of the Ten Commandments. It was Jesus' favorite commandment of the Old Law, to love one's neighbor as we love our own self. The man, however, was not content with that answer. He had kept these rules since his youth, he said. He wanted to do something more. "If you want to be perfect, go sell what you have and give to the poor and come follow me," Jesus told him. The man wasn't expecting that, so he walked away confused and disappointed. But Jesus didn't say he had to do that. It was merely an option if the man really wanted to be perfectly committed to God and close to Him in a special way.

Jesus' answer, however, should be a message for all of us. We all wonder what God expects us to do with our money, especially given that the possessions we accumulate are far more than what we need or could ever use. Material riches are no different from any talent or gift we may have. God did not put us on earth and give us these gifts just for ourselves. He has shared with each of us part of Himself and His riches, so we can be His instrument in sharing with others who are in need spiritually or materially. When God gives us gifts it is not to build up our riches just for ourselves and our families. He honors us by allowing us to be His Hands and Feet and Heart to people who are in dire straits, and to better the community in which we live, but all that we give comes from the richness He has bestowed on us. If there are people who are starving and suffering among us, it is we who have to answer to God. When we approach Him in the end, He will ask us not how much we made but how much we gave away. And we can't say to Him, "I knew that if I gave away to others, they would only waste it." For then He will say to us, "What did you do with all that I shared with you?" And we will lower our heads in shame. And we know it won't do to say, "We made our families rich on your treasures."

The rich man in the story apparently was kind to people in need, as he told Jesus, but Jesus offered him the possibility of a more perfect life: giving up all his possessions to benefit the destitute and then coming to be one of His special followers. It is only to the apostles that Jesus used those words, "Come, follow me!" The man was offered a special place in Jesus' friendship. Even Jesus felt sad that the man walked away, because He could see that there was goodness in the man.

I think God calls each of us to something special, but

when most of us think it over we calculate all those things dear to us that we would have to give up, and we end up having a difficult time saying yes to God, because we can't imagine our life with God being very much fun. What we don't realize is that life becomes an exciting adventure when He is our partner and an intimate part of our life.

"Why Was This Not Sold to Help the Poor Rather Than Waste It on Him?"

Six days before the Passover Jesus came to Bethany, where Jesus had raised Lazarus from the dead. They cooked supper for him and Martha served, while Lazarus with the others reclined at table with him.

Mary took a pound of ointment, made of very costly genuine nard, and anointed the feet of Jesus and wiped them dry with her hair. The whole house was filled with the odor of the ointment. One of the disciples, Judas Iscariot, who was about to betray him, said, "Why was this not sold for three hundred denarii, and the money given to the poor?" He said this not because he cared for the poor, but because he was a thief and stole money from the common purse, which he took care of. Jesus said, "Leave her

> *alone, that she may keep it for my burial. The poor*
> *you have with you always, but you do not always*
> *have me."* JN 12:1–8

WE ARE SHOCKED AT JUDAS'S CONTEMPTUOUS AT-
titude toward the use of this costly ointment on
Jesus. What a waste! But strangely enough I have heard
people say the same thing so many times through the
years. I will never forget one incident in particular. A man I
had known for years, a rather cynical kind of fellow, had
just come back from a trip to Europe. He and his wife had
spent a good amount of time in Italy. He couldn't wait to
tell me about his experience there. "Every place you go in
Italy, even the little villages, you see these beautiful big
churches. They are all throughout the country. What a
waste! Why didn't the Church use all that money to help
the poor instead of wasting it on those big piles of stone?"

I have to admit I did not take that comment very well. I
said, "You know, I heard a comment like that once before.
The fellow asked why the woman in the Gospel anointed
Jesus' feet with a very costly ointment. A dinner guest,
seeing this, commented, 'What a waste! Why wasn't that
ointment sold and the money given to the poor?' To Judas's
way of thinking, using the ointment on Jesus was a waste.

All those churches you saw throughout Italy were not built by the Church. They were built by the poor villagers, who had nothing else to give God but the fruit of their talents. They cut the rocks. They designed the buildings and everyone joined in to construct those beautiful architectural masterpieces as their way of expressing their faith and gratitude to God. Those churches are beautiful expressions of faith. Today such structures would be considered a waste, but not because we are concerned about the poor. The ones who say that kind of thing are rarely generous to the poor. They just love their money, like the man in the Gospel."

A few weeks ago some friends of mine visited another friend's church. They were shocked to hear the preacher talking about monks in monasteries and commenting that there is no place for that kind of thing in Christianity—people who don't talk and have little to do but engage in religious practices, like fasting and discipline. The visitors, who were Catholics, were deeply offended, and rightly so. Those monks don't waste their time. Many of them have previously worked as doctors, lawyers, architects, and businessmen who had had everything and decided that there must be more to life than just material success. So they joined a very strict order where they could spend the rest of their lives in the intimate presence of God, speaking little so they could spend most of their time meditating on spiritual things, and on Jesus' life. Their schedule at the monastery is rigorous: prayers at 4 a.m., then again at 6 a.m., and then daily Mass, and breakfast—and again prayers at 9 a.m., and again at noon. In between they do their assigned tasks—some are authors of spiritual books, like Thomas Merton; others work on the farm or make the products the monks sell to support the monastery. Then they have prayers again at twilight and then night prayers, praying all of the 150 Psalms each week, plus Bible readings at each prayer session and meditation at various times. Their whole life is centered on God, meditating, as it says in Scripture, on the things of God, day and night, praying not just for themselves but for the whole world. To some, spending one's life centered on God is a waste. What a disappointment they will have when they go to heaven and realize they will have to spend their whole eternity with God.

One Moment of Glory

When they drew near to Jerusalem and came to Bethphage on the Mount of Olives, Jesus sent two disciples, telling them, "Go into the village opposite you, and immediately you will find an ass tied, and a colt with her. Loose them and bring them to me. If anyone says anything to you, tell him the Lord has need of them, and immediately he will send them." Now this was done so that what was spoken through the prophet might be fulfilled: "Tell the daughter of Sion, 'Behold, your king comes to you, meek and seated upon an ass, and upon a colt, the foal of a beast of burden.'"

So the disciples went and did as Jesus had directed them. They brought the ass and the colt, laid their cloaks on them, and helped him to mount.

Most of the crowd spread their cloaks on the road; others cut branches from the trees and spread them out along the road. The crowd that went before him and the crowd that followed kept crying out, "Hosanna to the Son of David! Blessed is he who comes in the name of the Lord! Hosanna in the highest." When he entered Jerusalem, the whole city went wild with excitement, and questioned, "Who is this?" The crowd kept on telling them, "This is Jesus the prophet from Nazareth in Galilee." . . .

And the blind and the lame came to him in the Temple, and he healed them. But the chief priests and the scribes, seeing the spectacular deeds he was doing and the children crying out in the Temple, "Hosanna to the Son of David," were incensed, and said to him, "Don't you hear what they are saying?" And Jesus said to them, "Yes, have you never read, 'Out of the mouths of infants and babes at their mother's breast, you have perfect praise.'" And leaving them he went out of the city to Bethany and stayed there. MT 21:1–11, 14–17

I AM JUST BEGINNING TO UNDERSTAND SOME OF THE wide spectrum of messages Jesus sent out on that first Palm Sunday. The people, especially His apostles, had been pressuring Jesus to declare Himself, to reveal His identity as the long-awaited Messiah. It seems clear to me finally what Jesus did on that day, and how much He revealed on that fateful day. He perfectly orchestrated every one of His moves, and everything He did had a message, a clear message, not in words, but in powerful symbolism.

In entering Jerusalem seated on a donkey, Jesus' message was loud and clear: "Yes, I am the Messiah." The people immediately responded by showing Him all kinds of honor, singing hymns to the Messiah, and in joyful triumph waving olive branches, as they triumphantly marched along with Him toward the gate that leads directly to the Temple mount. The huge crowd lost all their fear of the religious authorities who had forbidden anyone to manifest approval of Jesus, especially in public. Even the children sensed the majesty of the occasion and proclaimed in song their welcome to the one sent by God.

As Jesus entered the courtyard of the temple, he was sickened by the mob scene, resembling the Chicago stockyard with animals all over, dropping their filth on the sacred approach to God's house, and people haggling over prices for the animals to be sacrificed. Jesus was furious, and in a most powerful statement of His real identity He picked up a length of rope, used it as a whip to stampede the animals, and turned over the tables of the money changers, declaring, "It is written, 'My house shall be called a house of prayer, but you have made it a den of thieves.' " It is interesting that Jesus identified the Temple not as His Father's house but as "My house." He could have made a slight change in the prophetic quote and said, "My Father's house," but He seems to be making a powerful statement here that He and His Father are one.

Strangely, there seem to have been a number of blind and crippled people in the vicinity of the Temple, and they cried out for Jesus to heal them. And He did. And the children were still singing His praises, "Hosanna to the Son of David." The chief priests and the scribes were furious. They could not permit this spectacle to continue. The manifestation of Jesus' divine power and His favor with Yahweh could not be allowed in front of all these people. The religious authorities demanded that Jesus make the children stop singing. Jesus' response is delightful: in paraphrase, "Even little children in their innocent honesty recognize the truth, a truth so obvious that even if I stop their singing, the dead stones themselves would speak out the truth, the truth you refuse to see."

Jesus left the authorities standing there speechless and paralyzed. They didn't dare order His arrest. The people would have killed them. Jesus just walked away disgusted, but He had made a powerful statement: He let them know that God Himself had come to visit His people at His own house, but the very people who should have been prepared to welcome their Host did not recognize Him.

As He walked away, the chief priests, while overwhelmed by the experience, knew that they could not let this proceed. There was too much at stake. This upstart, who now spoke of Himself as being one with the Divine Being, had thrown the populace into near frenzy. If the Romans heard of this, as they might have already, they would take away what little authority the religious leaders still had, and all would be lost. The chief priests then began to plot their strategy to rid themselves of this nuisance once and for all.

Their Last Supper Together

And when the hour came he sat at table, and the apostles with him. He said to them, "I have so eagerly desired to eat this Passover with you before I suffer, for I tell you I shall not eat it again until it is fulfilled in the Kingdom of God." And he took a cup, and when he had given thanks he said, "Take this and share it among you, for I will not again drink of the fruit of the vine until I drink it anew with you in the Kingdom of God." And he took bread, and when he had given thanks, he broke it and gave it to them, saying, "This is my body which is given for you. Do this in remembrance of me." And likewise the cup after supper, saying, "This cup which is poured out for you is the new covenant in my blood." LK 22:14–20

W HAT DOES JESUS MEAN WHEN HE SPEAKS THESE words to the apostles, "I have so eagerly desired to eat this Passover with you"? How could he have been eager for this his last night to be upon him, knowing that on the next day he will die?

Yet he was looking forward to that night. Why? How do you pry into the mind of a God? What human would be eager to celebrate his last supper? It is hard for us to understand how Jesus could be so happy about the arrival of his last night alive. Even writing about it is heartbreaking.

I suppose it is much akin to the arrival of the day a confessor for the faith is giving his or her life to God as a martyr. The ninety-five-year-old Ignatius of Antioch looked forward to his martyrdom with joy, even though he knew it meant being torn apart by wild animals.

Jesus knew that he was going to be surrounded later that night and all the next day by his enemies, like a pack of wild dogs, as described in the Twenty-third Psalm. What Jesus was looking forward to was the realization that the chief purpose of his coming to earth had finally arrived: to give his life for the salvation of the whole human race, from our first human parents to the last person at the end of time.

This night had been on Jesus' mind for nearly six

months, ever since the multiplication of the loaves and fishes, which so excited the crowd that they wanted to acclaim him king and Messiah that very evening. That night, however, was for Jesus merely a prelude to what he knew he was going to do the next day, which was promise to them the gift of himself as the food of their souls, the food of which the manna given in the desert to their ancestors was a mere symbol. The crowd that, on the evening before, was so impressed with the miracle of the multiplication of the bread and fish, were now appalled at his even suggesting that he would even think of giving them his flesh and blood as food for them to eat and drink, especially when he emphasized three times that what he said he meant. What he did not tell them was how he would give them this gift of himself in a way that would make sense.

Now, on this last night of his life, on the occasion of the official sacrificial meal of the Old Covenant, he manifested the fulfillment of that promise. After having eaten the sacrificial Passover lamb, Jesus instituted the official sacrificial meal of the New Covenant by taking a loaf of unleavened bread and, after giving thanks to his Heavenly Father, passing it around to the apostles, telling them, "Take and eat; this is my body which will be given up for you." Then, taking the cup of wine, he offers it to them with the words, "Take and drink this, all of you; this the cup of my blood, the blood of the New and everlasting

Covenant, which will be shed for you for the forgiveness of sins. Do this in memory of me."

What seemed so impossible for the crowd to understand six months earlier now seemed so simple and so reasonable. "This bread is now my body, the wine is now my blood, which I give to you." In some way a miracle had taken place. He said it was His body and His blood, but did not say how He was present in that bread and wine. And just like so many things Jesus told us that are hard to understand and believe, so here we cannot understand how He is present. Some Christians, even today, still react in the same way the unbelieving crowd reacted; they cannot accept it, and do not believe what Jesus insisted he meant: "My body is real food, and my blood is real drink."

Even though we will never understand how Jesus is present, we know that Jesus created a new kind of presence, different from the presence of God throughout the universe, a presence that He meant to be for us a comfort and a joy in our difficult lives here on earth, the kind of presence in which we can experience in a beautiful, intimate fashion the tenderness of His love for us, when we gather as a family to offer our Eucharist, our thanks to him for all the wonders of His redemption of our lives and accepting us again as part of God's family.

What is surprising about this celebration of the first Eucharist is that Jesus enacted it while Judas was still present. It was only afterward that Judas left to betray Jesus. What is significant is that He offered Judas the Eucharist, knowing that Judas had already committed in his heart the horrible sin of betraying Jesus.

The other apostles finally realized what Jesus was doing for them, sharing in some way His life in a very intimate and profound way, which they still could not fully understand, and which would mean more and more to them as they shared this mystery of faith with those who later accepted Jesus as their Savior.

As Christians later on in the first century and the beginning of the second century gathered together for their sacred service, it was not for Scripture readings, but for the sacred meal, the Eucharist, which was the reenactment of Jesus' meal with the apostles. It wasn't just a memorial, it was the *reenactment* of what Jesus did at the Last Supper that kept alive the memory of what He had given to us. And they would sacrifice their lives to bring the Eucharist to the Christians in the Roman prisons waiting for their approaching martyrdom.

The Sad Last Night

Jesus went forth with his disciples to a country place called Gethsemane, and he said to his disciples, "Sit down here while I go yonder and pray." And he took with him Peter and the two sons of Zebedee, and he began to be saddened and exceedingly troubled. Then he said to them, "My soul is sad even unto death. Wait here and watch with me." Going forward a little, he fell on his face and prayed, "Father, if it is possible, let this cup pass from me, yet not as I will but as you will." Then he came to the apostles and found them sleeping. He said to Peter, "Could you not watch with me one hour? Watch and pray that you may not enter into temptation. The spirit indeed is willing, but the flesh is weak." Again a second time he went away and prayed, saying, "My

> *Father, if this cup cannot pass away unless I drink it,*
> *your will be done."* MT 26:36–43

> *His sweat became as drops of blood running*
> *down upon the ground. And rising from prayer he*
> *came to the disciples and found them sleeping for*
> *sorrow.* LK 22:44–45

> *Judas also knew the place, as Jesus often gathered*
> *there with his disciples. It was not long before Judas*
> *came with the cohort and attendants from the chief*
> *priests and Pharisees, armed with lanterns, torches,*
> *and weapons.* JN 18:2–3

MANY IMPORTANT INSIGHTS INTO JESUS' INNER life are revealed in these lines. Because we know that Jesus is God, it is frightening to see Him overwhelmed with sadness and grief, and the human part of His being on the verge of panic. If God panics, how can we not shudder with horror and not be overwhelmed with dread? Even the apostles, who for the longest time could not believe what Jesus was talking about when He warned them of His approaching death and the horrible circumstances surrounding it, finally realized it was about to happen. They were so overcome with the immensity of this tragic ending, as tough as they were, they could not face it, and like some people in similar situations they retreated by falling asleep. So while Jesus was going through this horrible torment, they fell asleep, not because they chose to, but because their conscious soul could not bear to witness what was happening. Jesus had called them to be close to Him because He felt so alone, but they were unable to be of any comfort or support to Him. When, trying to distract Himself, He broke away from His prayer and went to the apostles for comfort, He found them sound asleep. They meant well, Jesus thought, but though "the spirit is willing, the flesh is weak," so He went back to commune with His Father in heaven for comfort and strength.

While Jesus was in Gethsemane, He made a startling remark: "This is the hour of the power of darkness." Over the years I just *read* that line, not realizing the import of what Jesus was saying. It was only lately that I finally understood what He was saying, something very hard to believe. If it was the hour of the power of darkness, what He was saying is that at that moment Satan had been allowed to be victorious, to defeat God's plan of redemption that the Father had so carefully designed for all those thousands of years, the beautiful plan for the thousand years of the Messianic reign of peace and prosperity for His chosen people and for the world. While I was talking about this recently I finally realized that God Himself had to struggle against evil. Satan had managed to cunningly pervert human souls so that they would side with him in fighting God and perpetrating evil. In this struggle between God and Satan, Satan was able to turn God's chosen religious teachers into tools to destroy Yahweh's plans for the redemption of His people. I was beginning to realize what Jesus meant when He told the scribes and Pharisees, and the priests, that God was not their father, but they were truly the children of their father, and their real father was Satan. He was telling them that they were doing the work of Satan in cooperating with hell itself to frustrate the beautiful plans God has for His chosen people and for the whole family of God on earth.

In the garden, this all became reality. What Jesus was struggling with, and the Father and the Holy Spirit along with Him, was how to deal with Satan and the powers of evil. God could not violate the free will He gave us, but Satan was allowed to pervert the free will of God's chosen teachers and make them his unwitting allies. That was why Jesus told the apostles to pray hard lest they succumb to Satan's trickery.

"What do we do now?" The Holy Trinity now has to contemplate its options. Satan cannot win the war, just this battle, perhaps. As God never runs out of options, God had a strategy that would totally frustrate Satan. Let

Satan's evil plans take their course, Jesus, the Father, and the Spirit decided. In the very act of His Son's becoming a victim of evil, He would in turn offer Himself to His Father as the innocent victim in atonement for the sins of the whole human race from the beginning of time to the end of time. This stupendous act of love by the Son of God would then forever be graphic evidence of the immensity of God's love for His human family, proof that His Son was willing to undergo humiliating suffering and torture and shameful death to win our salvation and eternal life with God.

What was lost when the religious leaders failed to recognize the Messiah was what God had originally planned for His people. If the priests and teachers had recognized their Messiah and presented Him to the Jewish people, a thousand years of the Messianic reign of peace and prosperity would have been ushered in. They would have then introduced the Savior, "the Light to the Gentiles," to the pagan peoples, who would have accepted Him. The promise of God to Abraham would have been fulfilled: "You will be the father of many nations." The Jewish religion would have reached the zenith of God's plan for the transformation of the human race into one family, with the center of this worldwide worship of Yahweh being still in Jerusalem. And I wonder, if that had happened, would God have had another way of redeeming us without His Son having to die for us? That is a thought that crosses my mind so often, because the way things turned out, He was the victim of people's meanness.

That wonderful plan was not to be, but God would not be frustrated. The love manifested by Jesus' willingness to die for all of us won the final victory over evil and established the Kingdom of God in such a way that Satan could never again interfere. The Kingdom of God would be planted in each human soul that opened itself to salvation. Satan would never be allowed to enter the depths of that soul. The new Messianic kingdom would be forever beyond Satan's reach. Only those souls who refused to allow God entrance into their lives would still be vulnerable to Satan's evil plans.

So when we get frustrated with the evil in this world we cannot blame it on God. He gave us free will. And because of all the evil things His creatures do to frustrate His loving plans for us, He has to continually create options to bring good out of the messes we make. Even though we ourselves may suffer much from the evil of others, in the end God will always triumph and our final destiny will be glorious beyond our dreams.

Sunrise on a Dark Night

Early Sunday morning, when dawn was breaking, Mary of Magdala went to the tomb, and seeing that the stone had been rolled back, ran and came to Simon Peter and the other disciple whom Jesus loved, and told them, "They have taken away the Lord from the tomb, and we don't know where they have put him."

Peter and the other disciple went out and made their way to the tomb. The two of them were running together, but the other disciple ran faster than Peter and was the first to reach the tomb. Stooping down, he saw the burial cloth lying there, but he did not go in. Then Simon Peter came along behind him and went in. He also saw the burial cloth, and the cloth that they had used to cover his head, lying

*not with the burial cloth, but rolled up by itself.
Then the other disciple, who had been the first to
arrive at the tomb, went in. He saw all this and believed. But as neither of them yet understood the
prophecy that he was to rise from the dead, these
disciples went back home.*

*Mary, however, stood crying outside, and in her
tears she stooped to look into the tomb, and she saw
two heavenly messengers in white seated where Jesus' body had lain, one at the head and one at the
feet.*

"Woman, why are you crying?" they asked her.

*"They have taken away my Master," she told
them, "and I do not know where they have put
him."*

*No sooner had she said this than she turned
around and saw Jesus standing there, but she did
not know it was Jesus.*

*"Woman," he said to her, "why are you crying?
Who is it you are looking for?"*

*Thinking it was the gardener, she said to him,
"Please, sir, if you moved him, tell me where you
have put him and I will take him away."*

"Mary," Jesus said.

*She turned around and exclaimed in Hebrew,
"Rabbuni!" (which means "Dear Teacher").*

> *"Don't touch me," Jesus told her, "because I have not yet gone to the Father. But go to my brothers and tell them, 'I am going back to my Father, and to your Father, to my God, and to your God.'"*
>
> *So Mary of Magdala went and reported to the disciples, "I have seen the Master," and related all that he had told her.* JN 20:1–18

IT TAKES GREAT FAITH TO READ THIS ACCOUNT OF the Resurrection of Jesus and not have a thousand questions. Even approaching this account with faith it is hard not to have questions, serious questions. Cynics through the ages have attacked the Resurrection from so many angles it is difficult not to be conscious of their constant barrage of snide comments on this central event in Christianity. John's Gospel grounds the event on a solid base of reality. John was no dreamer. For such a devoted follower of Jesus, he could be brutal and also cunningly worldly. I was convinced of this because of all of Jesus' followers John alone had the brashness to wheedle his way into the intimate circle of the high priest's family, which got him entrance into the high priest's palace when Jesus was being tried by the Sanhedrin. His same contacts after the Resurrection made it possible for him to find out what the guards at Jesus' tomb told the chief priests about what had happened at the grave site that morning: how the earth had shaken; how when the huge stone sealing the entrance had fallen away the tomb was already empty, with the burial cloths lying on the ground, indicating that the body had earlier disappeared seemingly through the solid rock. That explained why so many Pharisees, and priests as well, became disciples after the Resurrection. How could they not after the witness of the guards?

John talks about Mary of Magdala visiting the tomb. He doesn't mention the other women who accompanied her, as related in the other accounts. Surprised that the body had disappeared, and that the guards were nowhere to be seen, she immediately ran back through the city streets to the other side of town where the apostles were hiding from fear. "The Master's body has been taken. It is gone." Not knowing what to make of it, Peter and John ran out to the tomb and found it just as she had said. John reached the tomb first. Peter, who apparently was short and stocky, was out of breath, so John waited for him to catch up and let him enter the tomb first. They found the tomb empty as Mary of Magdala had said, and the shroud lying on the floor. The cloth that had covered His head was rolled up and lying on the slab where the body had lain. All that John says is that they believed, probably what Mary of Magdala had told them, but not about a Resurrection. So, not knowing what to make of it all, they went back home.

Mary of Magdala, who apparently had followed them out to the tomb, stayed there and was well rewarded. Jesus must have been present nearby during the whole episode, but unseen. Why did He keep Himself hidden from Peter and John? Did He still have things to teach them before He would show Himself to them? Was He disappointed with their behavior and lack of faith after He had tried so hard to prepare them for everything that was to happen? Whatever the reason, Jesus let the whole day pass before He would have anything to do with them. As soon as Peter and John left, beautiful things took place; there was Mary of Magdala's vision of the strange messengers inside the tomb, and the stranger in the garden who turned out to be Jesus Himself. Mary of Magdala was well rewarded for her devotion and her love; her loving attitude was so different from the cold, detached attitude of Peter and John, who saw no reason to hang around that precious spot and meditate on what could have happened. One finds it hard to believe these men could be so dense and detached, or maybe they were fearful that someone might catch them there with the body gone and they might be liable to arrest. Had they no curiosity, no little spark of faith that what Jesus had promised about rising on the third day might actually happen? One can begin to understand the difficult time Jesus had in trying to penetrate their thick minds.

How Jesus came to visit his apostles that evening is interesting, as you will see in the next snapshot of Jesus' escapades on that Easter day.

Surprise!

Two disciples were going that very day to a village named Emmaus, which is sixty stadia from Jerusalem. They were talking to each other about all the things that had happened. It came to pass while they were conversing and arguing that Jesus himself approached and went along with them, but their eyes were prevented from recognizing him. He said to them, "What are you discussing as you walk along, and why are you so sad?"

One of them, named Cleophas, answered and said to him, "Are you the only stranger in Jerusalem who does not know the things that have happened there in these days?" "What things?" he said to them.

And they told him, "Concerning Jesus of

Nazareth, who was a prophet, mighty in work and word before God and all the people; and how our chief priests and rulers delivered him up to be sentenced to death, and crucified him. We were hoping that it was he who should redeem Israel. Yes, and besides all this, today is the third day since these things took place. And certain women of our company, who were at the tomb before it was light, astounded us, and not finding the body, they came, saying they had seen a vision of angels who had said that he is alive. So some of our company went to the tomb and found it as the women had said, but him they did not see."

And he said to them, "O foolish ones, so slow of heart to believe all that the prophets have spoken! Did you not know that the Christ would have to suffer these things before entering into his glory?" And beginning with Moses and with all the prophets, he interpreted to them all the Scriptures referring to himself.

As they drew near the village to which they were going, he acted as if he was going on. They urged him, saying, "Stay with us, for the day is almost over and it is almost evening." He went inside with them and reclined at table with them. Taking a loaf of bread, he blessed it, broke it, and handed it to them.

And their eyes were opened and they recognized him. He then vanished from their sight. They said to one another, "Were not our hearts burning within us as he spoke with us on the road and explained the Scriptures to us?"

They left immediately and returned to Jerusalem, where they found the apostles gathered together and those who were with them, saying, "The Lord has risen indeed, and has appeared to Simon." And they themselves related what had happened on the journey, and how they recognized him in the breaking of the bread. Lk 24:13–35

WHILE THEY WERE STILL TALKING, JESUS suddenly appeared in the midst of the darkened room. He could have just knocked at the door, but no, He seems to have been enjoying this newfound ability to penetrate matter. So He just appeared in the room, scaring the wits out of the apostles and the others. John says they were all panic-stricken and thought they had seen a ghost. They just stood there gaping at Him. "Why are you so upset and why do you still have doubts? See, look at me! Look at my wounds! Touch me and see. A ghost does not have flesh and bones. Do you have anything to eat?" And they gave

Him a piece of roasted fish and honeycomb and He ate it. "Can a ghost eat?" When they were convinced it was really Jesus, He reproached them for their lack of faith and their obstinacy.

That first Easter Sunday was finally over. After forgiving the *apostles* for *their* obstinacy and lack of faith, He then breathed on them and gave them the gift of the Holy Spirit, and with that the power to forgive the sins of others. They would not be the only disciples who would be deficient in their loyalty to the Lord. They too would need to receive His forgiveness and with that His peace and reconciliation with His family.

This power to forgive sin that Jesus gave the apostles is so isolated from the rest of the Resurrection story, it is possible the apostles did not fully understand its meaning until later on. As it turned out, when a group of Christians later abandoned their faith when faced with martyrdom and then repented and asked to be forgiven, the apostles at first did not know what to do. While considering the problem, James reminded them of Jesus' words on Easter night: "Whose sins you shall forgive, they are forgiven." They then told the repentant apostates they would be accepted back and forgiven after performing a penance for their sin.

Later on reconciliation was extended to those who committed murder and notorious adultery.

Seeing Is Not Believing

Now Thomas, one of the Twelve, called the Twin, was not with them when Jesus came. The other disciples told him, "We have seen the Lord." But he said, "Unless I see in his hands the print of the nails, and put my finger into the place of the nails, and put my hand into his side, I will not believe."

After eight days, the disciples were again inside, and Thomas was with them. Jesus came in with the door still locked and stood in their midst. "Peace be with you!" he said. Then he said to Thomas, "Bring your finger here, and see my hands, and bring your hand here and put it into my side, and do not be so unbelieving, but now believe." Thomas answered and said to him, "My Lord and my God!" Jesus said to him, "You believe now, Thomas, because you

> have seen. Blessed are they who believe and have
> not seen." JN 20:24–29

THE APOSTLES REMAINED IN JERUSALEM FOR AT least a week after the Resurrection before returning to Galilee. It was during that time that Jesus appeared to the apostles again, this time for Thomas's benefit. Where Thomas was during that whole week there is no way to tell. But he must have heard the news of Jesus' reappearance at some time during the week. In spite of that, he still did not believe and was quite adamant about it. This and other self-incriminating statements the apostles made in their stubbornness and refusal to believe all that Jesus had previously told them about the Resurrection reinforce our realization that the Resurrection was not something concocted by the apostles. They certainly did not paint a very flattering picture of themselves, and even the nasty comments they made about the whole story they heard from the women did not enhance their image.

I suppose they were no different than we would be today. I am sure many of us would find the Resurrection hard to believe, even if we were close to Jesus. Such a thing had never happened before in human history—that a person would rise from the dead under his own power.

Why should they believe it? Because Jesus promised it? They still did not know the true identity of Jesus. That He was a prophet and a special kind of prophet—this they could accept. But anything above that was beyond their ability to accept, much less comprehend. So when Jesus appeared to the Eleven again and immediately confronted Thomas, telling him to touch His wounds and put his hand into His side, Thomas was ashamed when he realized that Jesus was aware of his cynical remarks about His rumored Resurrection. "My Lord and my God" is his heartfelt way of telling Jesus he was sorry.

Are we any different? We have been taught so many things about our faith, about confessing our sins to another human being, about Jesus' Body and Blood being really present in Holy Communion, about not taking human life as a penalty for crime, about the necessity of helping the poor and forgiving others who have hurt us, about the Church being necessary for our salvation. It is not just loving Jesus and talking about Him that is important in our relationship with Him. We need to believe and embrace *everything* He taught. Most Christians don't accept that. "It doesn't make any difference what you believe; we're all going to the same place" is the comment you hear so often today. I wonder what Jesus would say if someone told Him that. Yet that is what many, if not most, Christians believe. I am shocked to hear so frequently people telling me that they don't believe in the real presence of Jesus in the Eucharist, especially given that they were taught differently in their childhood. So Thomas is no different from us. Yet Jesus did not give up on him. He picked him to be an apostle for a reason, and later on Thomas carried the faith all the way to India, and many places along the way, and eventually was martyred for his loyalty to Jesus.

There is still hope for us. Jesus never gives up. But we have to be sincere. Faith in everything Jesus taught is the touchstone of our loyalty. Making a commitment once we find the truth is essential. Few are willing to make that commitment because it means giving up cherished attachments and friendships.

Good-bye, but I Am Not Really Leaving

"And now I am going to him who sent me, and not one of you asks me, 'Where are you going?' But because I have spoken these words to you your hearts are filled with sadness. I, however, speak to you what is true, that it is necessary for me to leave, for if I do not go the Advocate will not come to you. If I do go I will send him to you. And when I send him to you he will convict the world of sin, of justice, and of judgment; of sin, because they did not believe in me; of justice, because I go to the Father and you will see me no more; and of judgment, because the prince of this world has already been judged.

"Many things I have to say to you, but you can-

> *not bear them now, but when he, the Spirit of
> truth, has come, he will teach you all the truth. He
> will not speak on his own authority, but whatever
> he will hear he will speak, and the things that are to
> come he will declare to you. He will receive of what
> is mine and declare it to you."* JN 16:5–14

THESE WORDS OF JESUS, AS WELL AS THE REST OF His discourse to the apostles at the Last Supper, were not just sentimental expressions of someone about to leave His friends forever. The words are loaded with important information about the future of the Kingdom of God on earth, which He was placing completely in the hands of these men who He knew were, on their own, totally inadequate for the job. He was assuring them that they would not be alone. He would not leave them orphans as he had said previously in Jn 14:18. He was promising them the Holy Spirit, the other Person intimately related to the Father and Himself. It would be the work of the Spirit to constantly remind them of all that Jesus had taught them, and to guide them in the future into an ever deepening understanding of Jesus as His message would unfold in the years to come. It is the Spirit's guidance that would ensure the faithful transmission of Jesus' teachings in their integrity until the end of time.

Although these words of Jesus were spoken to the apostles at the Last Supper, they had more meaning after the Resurrection and after Jesus' Ascension into heaven, when the apostles would truly be without Jesus' presence, and would have to recall and ponder what He had committed to their care, and the weighty responsibility He had placed upon them. But even though these words were addressed to them, their meaning is a source of comfort for all of us. Jesus will not abandon us. He is sending to all of us His Spirit, not a nebulous, vague sort of presence but a real and powerful Person, the Third Person of the Trinity who shares the Divine nature; the Holy Spirit, who will be present with us, to be the élan vital, the living force who will live within us as a friend and companion to mold the thinking and love of Jesus in the depths of our souls, fashioning the image of Jesus in our daily lives, so that in time the work of Jesus' redemption will be completed within each of us. The terms Jesus used with His human creatures are sometimes hard to believe, especially when it one day strikes us that this is the omnipotent God whose wisdom and power masterminded the creation of the universe. He refers not just to the apostles, but to us as well, as friends. Why would this God want such insignificant beings as ourselves to be His friends? That is almost impossible to comprehend. Yet He has made us such by His choice, not because of anything we have to give Him. Our response, once we get over the shock, should not be cyni-

cal, or full of doubt, but just gratitude. Because our friendship means so much to Him, we should gratefully accept
His friendship and make sure we try to be the best friends
to Him that we possibly can be, since our friendship is all
we have to give. Jesus then shares with us the Holy Spirit
to be our comfort, the Source of our strength, our Guide in
difficult times, and the Wisdom that will guide each of us
if we are willing to listen. While the work of the Holy
Spirit is to keep alive among the apostles, and those who
succeed them, all the things that Jesus taught, thus assuring the integrity of the message forever, it is also the mission of the Spirit to work in each of us at a personal level
to develop an intimacy with Jesus so His kingdom will become real in each of us.

Jesus may have left the earth, but He did not leave us
orphans. He sent the Holy Spirit to be with us. Along with
the Holy Spirit there is Jesus also, as well as His Father,
though the Holy Spirit now has the dominant role in the
evolution of the Church and of our personal lives. God
lives in the Church and in each of us. A saintly Carmelite
nun, who was also a concert pianist as well as a mystic,
said that our souls are a temple where God dwells. We
must learn to live there with Him.

The world is in ferment, bubbling constantly with the
powerful force of God's Spirit. Redemption did not just
happen and end. It is an ongoing process, an ever-growing
movement of God's grace working throughout the world

not only among Christians but among all peoples. God has given us the sacraments and all the helps in our religion, but He cannot be restricted to work only through those means. He is still free to work in the world and in the souls of people to whom we Christians have still not reached out. Just as the apostles were surprised to find that people who had not yet been baptized had been touched by the Holy Spirit without even knowing who the Holy Spirit was, so today the Spirit's healing love touches the lives of souls in anguish from natural disasters and mental illness and from the cruelty of ruthless human beings. People's hearts are always being prepared for God's redeeming and saving grace. The mystery of God's work in the world is His ability to work alongside the most horrifying evil and destruction. That is why we cannot become disillusioned with God, as if He has lost control. He is very much in control, but we must be perceptive enough to sift the horrible, almost universal evil from the living presence of the Holy Spirit working quietly, imperceptibly, and surely alongside us throughout every space and at every moment of each day and night. The Spirit is never far from any of us. Even though we may become depressed with the present state of affairs throughout society, God knows that His plan for the salvation of the world will not be frustrated, and that in time all will be righted and evil will be conquered and all the victims of human suffering and injustice will be vindicated and blessed beyond human measure.